CU00730935

MY LIFE'S
BATTLES

MY LIFE'S BATTLES

WILL THORNE

Foreword by Paul Kenny
Introduction by John Callow

Lawrence and Wishart London 2014

Lawrence and Wishart Limited
99a Wallis Road
London
E9 5LN

This edition © GMB 2014
Published in association with the GMB

The authors have asserted their rights under the
Copyright, Design and Patents Act, 1998 to be identified
as the authors of this work.

All rights reserved. Apart from fair dealing for the
purpose of private study, research, criticism or review,
no part of this publication may be reproduced, stored
in a retrieval system, or transmitted, in any form or by
any means, electronic, electrical, chemical, mechanical,
optical, photocopying, recording or otherwise, without the
prior permission of the copyright owner.

ISBN 9781 910448 090

British Library Cataloguing in Publication Data.
A catalogue record for this book is available
from the British Library

CONTENTS

ABBREVIATIONS

British Communist Party	Communist Party of Great Britain
Gasworkers' Union	National Union of Gasworkers and General Labourers
GMB	General, Municipal & Boilermakers Union
GMWU	General & Municipal Workers Union
PLP	Parliamentary Labour Party
ILP	Independent Labour Party
SDF	Social Democratic Federation
TUC	Trade Union Congress

ACKNOWLEDGEMENTS

Research for the new edition of this book was helped, enormously, by the staff at three, very different archives, which – collectively – are treasure troves for anyone interested in the history of the British and internal Labour Movements. Jeff Howarth and James Goddard, at the TUC Library housed in London Metropolitan University, and Lynette Cawthra, at the Working Class Movement Library in Salford, were of enormous assistance in providing images, and access to the union's early books and journals. In Amsterdam, Marien van der Heijden and Ella Molenaar at the International Institute of Social History not only made available to me Eleanor Marx's papers, and the gasworkers' journals but also provided expertise, help and a wonderful setting in which to work.

Sally Davison and Lawrence and Wishart – one of the great independent, radical publishers in Britain – have built upon tradition in order to create a vibrant and important range of studies of contemporary culture and politics. GMB is indebted to both Sally, and L&W, for their expertise and for working so hard to bring to fruition the new edition of *My Life's Battles* in time for the celebration of the union's 125th anniversary.

125 FIGHTING YEARS

SOMETIMES fact can be far more fantastical, far more gripping, and far more liberating than any work of fiction. Will Thorne's book is one of the first, real working-class autobiographies. It is a story that charts an individual's rise from child labourer to trade union leader; from semi-skilled stoker to Member of Parliament. It is the story of the birth of my own union, the GMB, and of the founding of the modern British Labour Movement. It is the story of strikes and street fights; of political victories that grew out of real political conviction, and which, as a consequence, had the power to reshape the world. But, above all, it is a story of hope.

The union helped Will Thorne to find his own voice, just as it has helped hundreds of thousands of others, since 1889, to find their own and to make life better for themselves, and their families, in spite of all the odds.

In 125 years, the GMB – the union Thorne founded amid the smoke and fires of the Beckton Gasworks – has almost come full-circle. We have returned to the principles that we were built upon: of organising and campaigning for social justice, of putting our own members first, and of existing to challenge and to change all that is wrong, and just plain rotten, in our society. Now, as then, we are afraid of no boss, and beholden to no government and no politician.

In terms of the world of work, and the balance of power between labour and capital, the parallels between Thorne's day and are own are apparent, and sometimes even chilling. It is ironic that the campaign for the Eight Hour Day – which features so strongly in this book – has come back onto today's agenda. Yet, where once we had to ensure that a limit was placed upon the maximum number of hours worked, we now find ourselves fighting for the outlawing of zero hours contracts and for workers to have the right to a fixed, minimum number of hours, capable of providing them with a living wage. The cards may have been reshuffled but the rules of the game remain the same, with the dice still loaded in favour of the rich.

Yet we are far from being disheartened. Will Thorne chose the title of his book well. He knew that progressive change was never going to be handed over, on a plate, by the wealthy and the powerful. It was all about the battle. It would have to be fought for every step of the way, and every hard-won gain would need to be defended, afresh, each day. And, when all was said and done, he was a pretty good general to have on your side.

Today's GMB is not about to step back from that fight and to let all that was accomplished by generations of Socialists to help make Britain a fairer and healthier place – not least through our NHS and our Welfare State – evaporate like mist upon the fields.

Of course times change, attitudes alter, and some of Thorne's language can be judged as rough and uncomfortable. He uses expressions that we would not countenance, today. But the GMB takes a 'warts and all' approach to its own history: it is what happened, and why, that is important to us – not what we would want, or wish, it to be. We deal openly with what troubles us, and celebrate all that is worth celebrating. And believe me, the life of Will Thorne and the story of the union that he created and led are well worth celebrating.

It is absolute common sense to take control of your own life: to organise yourself and your workmates so that you can obtain – fairly – a level of dignity, comfort and direction for the many that the few have always taken through greed, force or trickery.

This book works as a historical document but it works equally as a political and human one. I'd like to see it in the hands of every one of our union members, and being recognised across the wider Labour Movement. It tells us where we came from and how we built, out of nothing, from the grassroots up. It tells of survival, when everything in the armoury of the bosses and the state was thrown against our young union; and it tells of lasting achievement in our founding of the Labour Party, and of our growing strength – culminating in the election victory of 1945 – through which we have sought to guarantee work, health and welfare, as inalienable human rights that stretched from the cradle to the grave.

However, it also informs our present. It's about thinking and feeling – and, then, getting out and doing. It shows us what is possible and what great things have been, and still need to be, achieved. Best of all, though, it demonstrates that talk of positive change, tomorrow, can yet be accomplished – through a combination of collective effort, principle and vision – before the day is out.

The GMB is a proud union and one that I'm immensely proud to lead. That pride is drawn from all those battles won and from the raw courage shown in fighting for change and social justice, on so many different fronts, when the things that we now take for granted were first seen, in their true colours, through the vision of those magnificent warriors for Justice that we call Trade Unionists.

Paul Kenny, General Secretary GMB,
November 2014

WILL THORNE:

UNDER THE RED FLAG

On Sunday morning, 14 April 1889, several hundred men met outside the gates to Battersea Park, anxious to hear the latest news from their union. The Gasworkers' Union – the forerunner of today's GMB – had been founded at Beckton less than three weeks earlier, and its reach had now spread like wildfire across London, with branches formed – or in the act of being formed – at Canning Town, East Ham, Barking, Deptford and Rotherhithe.[1] These were casual labourers, the semi- or unskilled, who often joined the meetings immediately after carrying out 18-hour shifts in the retort houses, where they fed the furnaces that heated, lit and powered the metropolises of Victorian England – men who had been held to be too immiserated, too marginal, and too difficult to reach and organise by a Trades Union Congress that was still dominated by the skilled craft unions. They seemed to outsiders like the living embodiment of H.G. Wells's *morlochs*, an unseen – or at least unacknowledged – strata of the working class. They worked in vast retort houses, at the extremes of temperature, subject to sudden and unexpected fluctuations, from burning heat to swirling draughts, amid grit, coal dust and gas fumes, and for a take-home pay which provided only the bare necessities for survival until the start of the next week's pattern of shifts.[2] Theirs was a highly physical job that was only suited to fully grown men, who had to endure exhaustion, very long hours and appalling working conditions; and they also lived with the constant threat of unemployment, subject to bullying foremen who had the absolute right to hire and fire.

The Beckton gasworks was an enormous industrial conurbation, hacked out of 150 acres of marsh-
land on the Thames estuary, with its own rail and
road links to the capital, and employing some 3000
workers. Every morning a crowd of men, seeking
casual employment, would line up outside the rail-
ings on the 'Sewer Bank', to be judged and sifted,
sent home or hired, by the foremen. At the end of each
shift, weary stokers – who carried their lunch
wrapped in a characteristic red kerchief – would pass
out along the same 'Sewer Bank', past groups of
begging children, hungry for their scraps. Sometimes
they shared what they had with the youngsters, or
fed the company's emaciated ponies, corralled on the
other side of the track. Sometimes they themselves
had nothing left to give. One among that number was
Will Thorne. He was confronted each new day by the
realities of hard manual labour, of the sacrifices
needed in order to power and beautify London, and of
the disparity between those who had and those who
had not. He is remembered today because he refused
to allow himself to be ground down, and because he
undertook to change the conditions that were destroying those around him.

A young Socialist present at the meeting at Battersea Park would years later recall the impression made
that day by the Gasworkers' acknowledged leader.
Seemingly, he had appeared from out of nowhere to
give the men a voice, a direction, and above all a sense
of purpose and of hope. Will Thorne was, he recalled,
a 'slight and fine-drawn [figure] through the heavy
labour of his arduous calling':

> He came to the platform straight from the retort
> house with the murk of that fiery place burnt into
> his features. Round his eyes were dark rings of coal-
> grime, and his hands were, and are still, gnarled
> and knotted by the handling of the charging-tools.
> His voice, as I remember it, was not strong, and his

words were not eloquent, but his obvious sincerity was more ... convincing than fine phrases.[3]

Had William Stephen Sanders known Thorne, he would have realised that his hands had been disfigured not, as he supposed, by the blow-backs from the furnaces at Beckton, but by acid splashes when he had been little more than a child, making shells in a Birmingham munitions factory. However this was otherwise an extremely perceptive comment on the impact of Thorne's entry upon the political stage; it accurately located the source of his power not in rhetorical flourishes but in his ability to harness the sum of the men's grievances to a clear and practical programme that sought social and economic justice, through political and industrial action, in order to name and redress the source of all those wrongs.

Young, brave and charismatic, Will Thorne was a Marxist at a time when the TUC was dominated by political Liberals, and when the SDF – the first recognisably Marxist party in British history – was wary, if not downright hostile, towards the role played by the unions in the struggle for radical change. This made Thorne something of an anomaly, and a curiosity, within the British Labour Movement. It is certainly the reason that Stephen Sanders remembered him, years after the event. However, this was also what conferred upon him something of his strength, and gave him his particular insight and authority. He was not afraid to look at the 'big picture', to equate economic with political power, and to tell his members that they did not suffer purely by chance. For Thorne, the exploitation of working people was not incidental to the capitalist system but was built into its very fabric; it was essential to the survival of private ownership of production and distribution. Yet he did not speak in the language of balance sheets, bulletins or the soulless blueprints of Five Year Plans. He spoke in a language formed by his own experience of the world of work, and as a consequence was able to speak directly to, and for, those around him. As a result of this his union was built from the grass-roots up. It was rough, ready and sometimes – not least during its first congress – verging on the chaotic; but it was above all a success.

The union, founded one 'Sunday morning, on a piece of waste ground in the Barking Road', seemed to take everybody by surprise.[4] The bosses had not expected such solidarity and articulation of purpose; and the nascent Socialist Left was equally taken aback by this spontaneous radicalism on the part of trade unionists, a group whom it had tended previously to dismiss as being hopelessly reformist – tied to the coat-tails of the Liberal Party and largely incapable of revolutionary thought and action. Now the accounts in their own press told otherwise. 'A resolute agitation has been started amongst the gas stokers of London', ran one such report. 'It appears that the men are sick and tired of their slavery, and the fact that they have been forced to do one or two extra "draws" has made them rebellious'. By the end of July 1889 it was claimed that the union had swelled to 17 branches, representing 6000 members, and barely a month later it was said to have risen again, to encompass 22 branches and 'a membership of over 8000'.[5] These were days of feverish agitation, street corner meetings, weekend rallies and mass protests, with the frequent unveiling of newly painted silk banners, and the accompaniment of brass bands playing the *Marseillaise*. Gangs of men were spirited across the capital in hired carts, or 'brakes', which served as speaking platforms once a destination had been reached. Multiple meetings were held on the same day, with the intent of forming new branches. Thus, after one rally ended, on the Barking Road:

> … the next business was to get off to Kensal Green, and some 300 or 400 of the Beckton men jumped into their brakes dinnerless, on purpose to be there in time. From Canning Town to Kensal Green the

procession was headed by a mounted marshal and the [Stevedores'] band, and along the line of route cheers were occasionally given by knots of lookers on.[6]

In this heady, almost carnival-like atmosphere, almost anything – and everything – seemed possible. One breathless report, written for *Justice* in the summer of 1889, held that:

There seems every probability that the London gas workers will gain nearly all their demands. The directors have already expressed their willingness to grant them an eight-hour day at the present rate of wages. The union is still increasing in numbers [and] Comrade W. Thorne has been elected Secretary.[7]

At the same time, one gasworker told *The Labour Elector* about the difference that having a union made. 'Don't you see?', he asked the reporter. 'They was bullied and couldn't say their soul was their own afore. Now the foreman and engineers are getting frightened and treat them a little bit like men'.[8]

Yet nothing was conceded without a fight. The strike that convulsed Vauxhall was particularly brutal, with more than 600 police being deployed around the gasworks, many arrests, and more than 40 convictions of union men for assault and public order offences. As at Leeds, Thorne was targeted for rough treatment, being repeatedly punched by police and kicked down a flight of stairs.[9] At Beckton, two strike-breakers were hurled from a moving train; decades after the event an old stoker would recall the unnerving effect of the growl and wolf-whistles that arose from thousands of throats every time a contingent of police or blacklegs were spotted near the works. 'The Beckton stokers' howl', he said, was 'the most unearthly noise I have ever heard'.[10] Events reached a crescendo at Leeds in July 1890, when regular troops – line infantry and hussars –

were routed at the 'Battle of Wortley Bridge', after an ambush by Thorne's gasworkers and their families; and in October 1890 three infantry battalions stationed at Chatham were issued with live ammunition and made ready to occupy the Beckton gasworks, with tugs requisitioned to ferry the soldiers up the Thames to the landing stages at Beckton. Although, fortunately, the order to mobilise was never given, the event had profoundly concentrated the minds of the union's leaders, who were all-too-well aware that they were playing for very high stakes, and of the need for a political, as well as an industrial, strategy.

A concerned – if not downright jumpy – article in *The Times*, published on 6 October 1890, reported that Thorne and his comrades had decided that the best way to counteract the threat of military and police intervention was to gain a say in how the state was governed, by returning the union's own members to Parliament. In fact the union was already engaged in local government elections and the battle to win local vestries and school boards; their first electoral success had been registered a year earlier.[11] Barely seven months after the foundation of the union, William Watkinson, a gasworker, and J.W. Braund, his fellow SDF activist, had been selected by the Barking Branch of the National Union of Gas Workers and General Labourers to stand in the elections for the local School Board. They were both returned, topping the poll, and with a majority of more than 300 over their nearest rivals; these included the local clergyman, the justice of the peace, a captain of the volunteer force and the 'Landlord's' candidate.[12] Two members of the management of the Beckton Gasworks also stood in this election, but trailed in at the very bottom of the poll with only 244 and 133 votes respectively. This victory, and the others that followed in its wake, revealed an effective appreciation of the latent political power that resided within a union. The union's own journal strove to reinforce the point:

If the Trade Unions in each constituency – nay, if a
hundred or so of the electors would make it clear to
the candidate or member that unless he promised
to press forward an Eight Hour's Bill he would have
to do without their votes, they would pretty soon
find that he would do what they wanted. Only one
thing is necessary; they must make it plain that
they intend to carry out their threat, if he refuses to
give way they must carry it out.[13]

This strategy, to obtain political power for the
working classes, found expression in the election of
Will Thorne and Pete Curran to Parliament, in 1906
and 1907 respectively, and culminated in a position
whereby, at the founding conference of the Labour
Party, in February 1900, the Gasworkers' delegation
wielded a large, and potentially decisive, block of
votes.[14] It had more delegates than any other union or
Socialist Society, and claimed 13 seats – including
those occupied by Thorne, Curran, Clynes and Hayday
– to be set against the 7 held by the Independent
Labour Party; the 4 of the SDF and the Fabian Society's single delegate.[15] However, the roots of such formi-
dable organisation and these initial electoral gains lay
in the union's unique relationship with the founders of
the international socialist movement; and in its ability
to see the pursuit of political and economic power as
being intrinsic to the nature of trade unionism, rather
than a side-effect or adjunct. Thorne was instrumental in this process.

The successes of the Gasworkers – in ushering in
the climate of 'New Unionism'; in establishing the first,
durable, union to represent semi- and unskilled
workers (both men and women); and in its determination to promote an avowedly Socialist programme –
had quickly brought Will Thorne to the attention of the
leaders and theorists of international Socialism.
Indeed, the union's first rule book proudly declared
that the union's members 'have thrown in their lot in

the battle of labour against capital', and that poverty
and unemployment would never be eradicated while
trade was only pursued in order to maximise profits.
Recalling the threat of the imposition of martial law
upon Beckton in October 1890, Thorne reminded his
membership that: 'It has been contended that we are
too Socialistic: that the general officials of the union
were hostile to the Liberal Party ... [but] we are hostile
to any party that will use gunboats and soldiers
against the workers'. Furthermore: 'To be a trade
unionist and fight *for* your class during a strike, and
to be a Tory or Liberal and fight *against* your class at
election time is folly'.[16] At this point, no other British
union was so highly theorised. Certainly, no other
British trade unionist could claim the same confi-
dences and deep friendships with the leading figures
of European Social Democracy; Thorne numbered
among his friends and allies Frederick Engels, Eleanor
Marx, Wilhelm Liebknecht, Jean Jaures and Viktor
Adler. These and others offered a heady and exhilarat-
ing atmosphere for a young man who had the benefits
of neither education or birth; but Thorne was more
than willing to learn from the celebrated thinkers,
writers and propagandists whom he now knew and
worked alongside. Moreover, as his memoirs clearly
show, he enjoyed every minute of his career at the
heart of the Second International – until the guns of
August 1914 narrowed his own possibilities and swept
away its wider vision of workers united by their class
as opposed to their nationality.

The Great War certainly acted as a watershed in
Thorne's own career. He was – and in some respects
would continue to be – far too left-wing for the main-
stream of the Labour Party. Yet, as an anti-Bolshevik
Marxist he was equally unacceptable to the British
Communist Party, despite his close personal friendships with Eleanor Marx and Frederick Engels. Had
he died at any point between 1890 and 1898, he would
surely have been hailed as one of Labour's 'great lost

leaders', a man who had succeeded in forging a militant, working-class union that was seemingly a world away from the caution and moderation of the established TUC. As it was, his role as an active recruiter for the war effort in 1914-18, and his subsequent acceptance of a CBE, served to tarnish his reputation with the radical, and largely pacifist, Left; while his extraordinarily long service to both his union and the Parliamentary Labour Party – 44 years as General Secretary, and 39 years as a sitting MP – ensured that as the years went by a certain weariness crept into his relationship with his colleagues, together with the palpable sense that the 'grand old man' had gone on rather too long. This view was most forcibly demonstrated by the lacklustre, and frankly uncharitable, epitaph afforded to him by his successor, Charles Dukes, who delivered the funeral oration over the former General Secretary's grave in January 1946.[17] There is little room for ambiguity or wish fulfilment when appraising Will Thorne's life, character and objectives. He did not lose, he was never fatally betrayed, he did not choose to rush headlong towards martyrdom, and he was not fated to die tragically neglected, misunderstood or young. Tough, shrewd, capable of humour – and of self-deprecation – he came from and stood for the working class, in both its noblest and more discordant aspects.[18]

As a consequence, he has been denied a prominent place among the heroes of the Labour Movement – such as Aneurin Bevan, Keir Hardie, James Maxton, Tom Mann or Ellen Wilkinson – and has often been ignored, subjected to condescension, or seen as severely flawed. E.P. Thompson chose to air-brush him out of his account of the Leeds Gas Strike, in favour of an artisan who had only the slightest of connections to the dispute that Thorne had led.[19] His former protégé, J.R. Clynes, came close to patronising Thorne as 'a notable instance of the triumph over a complete absence of education'; and his official trade union biographers thought him paradoxical; 'well advised to have retired in 1924'; and 'though a Socialist ... no theoretician'.[20] Matters were not improved by the dramatisation of his early life, *Will of Iron*, which used *My Life's Battles* as its model and attempted to introduce Thorne to a younger audience. Unfortunately, the play seemed to revel in his years of poverty and brutal adversity, while singularly failing to make much out of his triumphs and ability to transcend the hand that had been dealt him as a child by a harsh economic system and a violent home-life.[21]

Yet Thorne clearly had a story that was worth telling, and in some ways it is surprising that he waited until 1925 to set about the task. It was probably intended to act as a coda to an already long and fulfilling career, for Thorne could not have known as he sat down to write *My Life's Battles* that he would have another eight years leading the union and a further twenty in parliament. Unlike J.R. Clynes's first autobiography (which had appeared long before) and Margaret Bondfield's account of her ministerial career (which came out much later), in Thorne's book the union and industrial struggles – as opposed to high politics – take centre stage.[22] The memoir was written immediately before the General Strike, during a period of marked uncertainty within the GMWU, when falling membership threatened defeat, dissolution or merger, and in such circumstances it is understandable that Thorne preferred to mainly concentrate on the 'heroic' early years of the gasworkers' struggle, when everything had seemed achievable; and to avoid the obvious, and unfavourable, comparisons that would inevitably be drawn with his – and the union's – present, and very much diminished, circumstances. Just as important, though, was his clear concern to write nothing that would reflect badly upon his own union, or to indulge in diatribes and the settling of old personal scores.

Thus, by any standards, *My Life's Battles* is a particularly generous, human and humane work. Thorne does not seek to disguise his estrangement from his eldest son, to hide his grief at the death of his children, or to pretend that he did not have favourites among them. He delivers credit where credit is due, name-checking Hutchins, Hobart and Ward as seminal figures in the creation of the union, when few by the 1920s within the union – or without – would otherwise probably have remembered them, or their contribution. Similarly, he downplays the seriousness of his early struggle with Ben Tillett for control of the union, and just how visceral the fight became.[23] Thorne did not scruple at destroying Tillett's limited but troublesome caucus within the London gasworkers; but he was not prepared to celebrate such ruthlessness, or to humili-ate beaten men. As a consequence, on the two occa-sions that he does single out individuals within the Labour Movement for censure, his words have much more bite and act to a far deeper and, indeed, devastat-ing effect. It is thus clear that he felt that Edward Aveling, whatever his services to the fledgling union – and they had been both significant and many – was responsible for the suicide of Eleanor Marx. Thorne might well have forgiven Aveling, a slippery and singu-larly unattractive figure, for being something of a *roué*; but he felt that in driving 'the greatest of contemporary women' to her death he was beneath contempt, and that he deserved no more than a rebuke before being forgotten.[24] Much more startling is Thorne's willing-ness, right at the end of his book, to reveal the way in which he had been thoroughly humiliated by Philip Snowden, on account of his lack of formal education. It is hard to imagine a current Labour Movement leader, or indeed any politician, being prepared to reveal so much of themselves, their hurt and raw emotion. Snowden's polish, and disdain, cut Thorne to the quick, and thinking of it had reduced him to tears in front of his own members. This was for two, conjoined, reasons. The first was that they recalled the sorts of patronising put-downs that Thorne had had to suffer throughout

his life, from the rich and educated. These could nor-
mally be brushed off easily but in this case there was
the second reason for distress; namely that this time
they did not come from a foreman, a boss, or a Tory MP,
but from one who was supposedly on his own side. This
felt like a betrayal, and it tapped into Thorne's worst
fears – that maybe, after all, his critics had been right
all along, and he really was unfit to lead the union he
had created. The fact that he had been the house guest
of Engels, the confidant and pupil of Eleanor Marx, and
a comrade-in-arms to Jaures, Bebel and Pieck, suddenly no longer mattered. All that he remembered –
almost a decade after the event he described – was the
sting of patrician disdain.[25] Perhaps, though, Thorne
took some comfort from Snowden's removal from the
pantheon of Labour Party 'worthies' after he betrayed
the PLP in 1931, and joined the National Government
alongside Ramsay MacDonald and the Conservatives.
Certainly, the union's own journal had great fun pillo-
rying the defectors in its pages as the new Gunpowder
plotters, to be mocked by small children and carried in
effigy to be burned upon the bonfires on 5 November.[26]
However, it is far more significant – and revealing of
Thorne's own personality – that the validation he
required to regain his composure and continue his conference speech was the trust and support of his own
membership, registered in their thunderous applause.

His pride, and capacity for self-definition, were
vested in his union. As a result, *My Life's Battles* is the
story of the rise of that union and of Thorne's forma-
tive experiences of work, first as a child labourer, then
as a young man among gangs of navvies – an experience of travel and the outdoors which he appears to
have particularly relished – and latterly on the factory
and retort house floor, in Birmingham and London.
Consequently, it stands as a particularly rich and
important source for social historians, and as a land-
mark in working-class autobiography and self-realisa-
tion. The narrative, effectively, ends with Thorne's role

in the Great War and his visit to revolutionary Russia in 1917; and the more detailed account of Thorne's career and the development of his union concludes even earlier, in the late 1890s. It barely touches upon either the formation of the Parliamentary Labour Party, or Thorne's own work as an MP. You will look in vain, among the accounts of conversations with Lady Astor and menu lists from his trip to North America, for the sense that he consistently stood on the Left of the PLP, and struck a far more radical figure in Westminster than either of his union colleagues, Curran and Clynes.

During his career as an MP Thorne introduced private members' bills on the introduction of a National Minimum Wage, the Eight Hour Day and the Nationalisation of the Railways. He championed secular education, free from religious interference, opposed the contributory principle in Lloyd George's National Insurance Bill – breaking the Labour Whip to vote against it – and declined a place on the Industrial Improvement Committee, in 1912, while Clynes readily accepted a seat on the same board. Outside Westminster, he campaigned on behalf of the unemployed, advocated the seizure and occupation of waste land by the poor and the homeless, and urged the starving to break open the bread shops and bakeries so that they did not go hungry.[27] But only the last of these initiatives finds its way into the pages of *My Life's Battles* – together with Thorne's hasty retraction which spared him a hefty prison sentence for sedition.

The strengths, weaknesses and omissions of Thorne's autobiography have done much to shape the way in which his own union, today's GMB, has viewed both its founder and itself. Most damaging to his reputation is the manner in which the excitement, pace and sense of achievement that dominate the first eight chapters suddenly tails off, over the next four, into a series of set-pieces and anecdotes. It may well be that, after experiencing Fordist methods of production and the sheer scale of endeavour and apparent plenty in the USA, Thorne's acceptance of Marxism had been fundamentally challenged, and thereafter sharply eroded. It is certainly the case that the prevalent view of Thorne as having over time become increasingly 'comfortable' and detached from the struggle for Socialism is grounded within the last sixty or so, fairly lacklustre, pages, of what is otherwise a gripping, highly original and fiery memoir.[28] However, the reality would seem to have been subtly different.

The unpalatable truth was that in 1925 Thorne did not preside over the same union – in terms of membership, occupational groups, leadership, symbolism and core ideology – as he had in 1889-90. The success of the Leeds Gas Strike had certainly ensured the union's survival, but it had also resulted in the grudging acceptance, by Thorne and his comrades, that the union was now engaged in a long-term struggle for radical change that would be measured in years, rather than in weeks or even days, as they had originally thought. Victories were harder to come by and far less spectacular, and the opposition – not least through the activities of William Collison's murky and extremely brutal National Free Labour Association of organised strike-breakers – was far more focused and self-confident. The management at Beckton could successfully appeal to the state for military help, while the trade depression that set in after the early 1890s made it far harder to recruit to the union. Thus Thorne described the situation prevailing at the South Metropolitan Gas Works, where the union had hardly made any inroads, as resulting from the practice whereby 'the man who reported a unionist in the works got half a crown and the unionist got the sack'.[29]

The biggest problem, however, centred on the retention of membership. Many of the gasworkers, believing that they had gained all the concessions that they had wanted or were ever likely to get, became increasingly unwilling to pay their union dues. As a result, Thorne was moved to write one of his most powerful appeals to his membership, in order to impress upon them the absolute necessity of paying their membership subscriptions:

> By keeping up your payments in the Union you make a determined protest against the low wages and long hours, which tend to keep the workers bent to the earth ... By fighting the present system which breaks men, women and children to the wheel of capitalism, you are every day building a happier and nobler future for your wives and little ones ... Do you think that if you leave the Union you will be able to maintain all your privileges? Do not be mistaken ... The Union is the sole protection of the workers against tyranny. It can get a rise in wages, shorter hours and better conditions of labour for all. But on one condition. The Workers must stand by their Union, and by each other, and beware of traitors in their camp.[30]

The unfortunate truth was that the haemorrhage in membership continued, unabated, leading to a breathtakingly high rate of turn-over in terms of districts, branches and membership. Some districts, such as Lancashire and Sunderland, continued to grow in numerical strength and political importance, right up to 1913; while others, such as London and Leeds, experienced proportionate decline. Most dramatically of all, the Dublin District – founded by Adolphus Shields and representing the second largest power base in the union, in 1891 – had by 1893 almost completely disappeared. It took hard and prolonged lobbying by the Swansea branch before South Wales was afforded its own district, in 1900, while the North of the principality was entirely subsumed by the growing might of Lancashire. A distinct Scottish district was founded in 1899, but had collapsed by 1908, and had to be re-founded in 1913.[31] These shifts in regional membership and organisation had a knock-on effect on the governance and outlook of the national union.

It is perhaps unsurprising that the period covered in most care and detail in *My Life's Battles* is the period of London's dominance within the union; for that also represented Thorne's own power base. As the union had initially been formed from London gas branches, it followed that its first Executive, in 1889, was drawn entirely from the capital; and that until its eclipse, in 1908, the National Executive doubled as the London District Committee. This had made good sense in the union's early days, when the district had acted as the organisational centrifuge, bolting on unattached branches – stretching at one point from Swansea to Nottingham – that, for reasons of size, location or conflicting interests, could not be subsumed within the nearest geographical district. However, this situation could not last for long. The union had, almost from the outset, sought to appeal to all general workers: Thorne had been astute in seeking to recruit among workers in brick-making, the building trades, quarrying, the docks and agriculture – especially those engaged in picking fruit and hops – whose patterns of seasonal, casualised work neatly dove-tailed with, and supported, the gasworkers' own. And the survival of the union through the trade depression from the mid-1890s to the early 1900s had been ensured by recruiting more widely, within new sectional groups of unskilled labourers – the building and cloth workers being the largest and most significant – 'who needed it for a time, and then dropped-out to be replaced by another group'.[32] This tendency was given its formal, if perhaps overdue, expression in 1916, when the union changed its name to the National Union of General Workers. At the same time, during the period around the turn of the twentieth century, London was losing its pre-eminent position within the union. In 1899 it had accounted for 35 per cent of the total membership, set against Lancashire's figure of just 10 per cent.

However by 1908 the situation had been reversed; with London accounting for 19 per cent of the national figure and Lancashire now at 23 per cent. It was not by chance that the biennial conference held in that year would prove to mark a sea-change in the union's organisation and political culture.

The previously dominant London block, unofficially led by S.J. Wright – and tacitly supported by Thorne – now found itself ranged against a growing and increasingly assured Lancashire district, under the command of the ambitious, and utterly ruthless, J.R. Clynes. On one side stood the older vision of Thorne's union, somewhat inefficient but largely tolerant, championing its elected weekly executive and the concerns of the rank-and-file. On the other stood Clynes, who had a gift for administration, and was capable of articulating the interests of a growing officer corps and harnessing a built-up resentment to London's dominance among the other districts. The result, at the Nottingham Conference, was the rout of the union's old guard and the personal, and political, triumph of Clynes. The rule book was comprehensively re-written, the weekly Executive meetings were abolished, and lay participation was gradually eased out of the union's internal democracy. From this perspective, it is possible to see the structures created by Clynes, after 1908, as lending the union its particular cultures, sense of moderation and unquestioning loyalty to the Labour Party leadership – features that dominated its development from that point up until the 1980s, and perhaps as late as 2005 – in contrast to Thorne's own more radical, militant and 'bare knuckle' approach.

The obvious question, of course, is why Thorne himself did not fight harder against this new dispensation. On occasion he was prepared to show his contempt for Clynes's cynical and heavy-handed methods, as he did publicly at the union's 1906 conference. For the most part, however, he seems to have been unwilling to venture his own position against a younger,

better organised and more intellectually polished
opponent, a man who controlled the union's adminis-
trative apparatus, and frequently seems to have held
Thorne himself completely spell-bound. The most dramatic, and arguably most significant, instance of
Thorne's bowing to the influence of Clynes occurred in
the run-up to the 1906 general election. At this time
Thorne continued to regard himself as an orthodox
Marxist, and as a member of the SDF he had baulked
at standing simply on a Labour Party ticket. He had
enjoyed considerable support within his West Ham
constituency for his decision to stand as the 'Socialist
and Labour' candidate, and was unequivocally backed
by the Countess of Warwick, who to a considerable
extent was bank-rolling his campaign. It was the dis-
approval of Clynes and a majority on the Executive of
his own union – not opposition from potential electors
in the constituency – that caused him to change his
position. This was a turning point, and one that
seemed to acknowledge an element of moral authority,
and greater political acumen, in the younger man.

In this light, Clynes's brief foreword to the first
edition of *My Life's Battles* can be seen as underlining
the nature of their relationship as it stood in the 1920s:
the President of the union – and also, let it be remembered, a former leader of the Labour Party – was
seeking to establish, before the world, his precedence
over, and magnanimity towards, the veteran General
Secretary. In actual fact, this introduction adds little
or nothing to the book; indeed, it simply quotes a
section of Thorne's own text over two long paragraphs.
For this reason, as well as for reasons of space and
economy, not to mention clarity – three introductions
to any re-issued memoir might seem somewhat overwrought! – Clynes's section has not been reprinted as
part of this new edition.

It would seem fair to suggest that from 1908 Thorne's
influence started to decline, and certainly by the 1920s
he was an isolated figure. In part this was simply due

to a force that none of us can hope to control: namely, the inexorable march of time. The union had been founded by a highly motivated and remarkably close-knit group of young men and women. However, the years had stripped away from Thorne's side many of his closest, brightest and most loyal confidants. Mark Hutchins had compromised himself through financial troubles; William Ward, despite enjoying Thorne's protection, had eventually proved himself too much of a liability – through his drinking and fighting – and been paid off; and Pete Curran died in tragic circumstances, burned out by over-work and the gulf between high ideals and harsh political realities. From the younger generation, the talented and charismatic Mary MacArthur had succumbed to cancer before she had a chance to shape the union, in the wake of a merger that she had helped to mastermind. Most damaging of all, Eleanor Marx's suicide had robbed Thorne of one of his closest advisers; it was Eleanor who had written much of the original rule book – the one that was replaced by Clynes in 1908 – and who had provided Thorne with so much of his political direction, as well as with important contacts within the international Labour Movement.[33] Genuinely popular with the rank and file members, who carried her portrait at the head of the Gasworkers' section on the first May Day march, in 1890, Eleanor had founded the union's first women's branches, and sought to bring succour, and a chance of victory, to the locked-out workers at Silvertown.[34] Her death deeply affected Thorne. A newspaper report recorded that, at her funeral:

> ... [his] words were rendered almost inaudible through the strong emotion by which he was affected, [he] spoke of the close friendship which he had enjoyed with [Eleanor], the devoted self-sacrificing work she had done on behalf of the Gasworkers and General Labourer's Union, and for the cause of the workers generally.[35]

With his old comrades from the London gasworks gone, and the tremendous reservoirs of intellectual support he could once have counted upon drying-up – through death, in the case of Eleanor Marx and Frederick Engels, and through ossification and a descent into jingoism, in the case of H.M. Hyndman – Thorne was thrown back upon his own resources, and into alliances with a new generation of altogether greyer and less inspired machine politicians, of the stamp of J.R. Clynes, Margaret Bondfield and Charles Dukes. Yet there was still undoubtedly fire in his belly. The union's journal was re-invigorated during the last years of his general secretaryship, to incorporate full-colour, modernist-inspired, artwork that consistently warned against the rise of fascism. (It was to be quickly and quietly tamed by his successor, Charles Dukes, who stripped-out most of its politics and replaced the striking graphics and topical cartoons with black-and-white photographs of the English countryside, and snapshots of ruined abbeys, rugged mountainsides, winding streams and stately homes.) When he was invited back to the Saltley Gasworks in Birmingham in 1929, 'to inspect the new plant and vertical retorts', Thorne showed the management that he had not mellowed in the slightest in his attitude towards them, and, as the union journal reported, though 'no doubt some of the work is higher [paced] than it used to be ... there are [still] many arduous and exhausting jobs, and Brother Thorne expressed himself freely on some things which should be done in the men's interests'.[36]

Retirement, unsurprisingly, did not sit easily with Thorne. He continued to write his parliamentary column for the union journal and retained a considerable level of prestige among both the officers and the rank-and-file. He remained an active constituency MP for West Ham; ironically, the wipe-out of the Parliamentary Labour Party in the election of 1931 actually enhanced his importance and usefulness. Where twelve union-sponsored MPs had sat before, now only he and Jack Jones were returned to Westminster. Clynes and Bondfield were among those who lost their seats. Thorne continued to press the union's position in parliament, railing against unemployment and styling Neville Chamberlain as a 'man with the kind of outlook that made the dockers come out [on strike] fifty years ago'. However, while he remained the union's leading force at Westminster, he no longer had any real say in the formulation, or implementation, of its policies.

Thorne's remarkable constitution saw him approaching his ninth decade with the same natural instincts, pride and gusto as an agitator and organiser that he had shown at Beckton more than half a century before. In April 1936 he wrote to his old comrade Tom Mann:

> This year I reach my 79th birthday, and I am pleased to say that during the summer months I carry on outdoor propaganda meetings at the corner of Beckton Road, in my rough and ready manner. I expound the principles of Social Democracy, on behalf of the West Ham Branch of the Social Democratic Federation, of which I am a fully paid up member.[37]

The Labour Party seems to have turned a blind eye to his dual party membership; and, on coming under attack from a young SDF firebrand, Thorne noted that he was by far the oldest member of his SDF branch and intended to remain in place until anyone dared expel him.[38] Unsurprisingly, they never did.

In his last years Thorne continued to live in the same house, 1 Lawrence Road, in West Ham, that he had occupied for more than four decades; sharing it now with his fourth wife, Beatrice – whom he had surprised his closest friends by marrying in April 1930 – and his unmarried, youngest daughter. The rooms were stacked with books, pamphlets and journals, his own papers and archives, and with the many gifts and honours that had been bestowed upon him, both nationally and internationally, during his long career. The two volumes of *Das Kapital* dedicated to him by Frederick Engels, and the small copper kettle left to him from Eleanor Marx's estate, were still in pride of place when the Blitz began to rattle the window panes and light up the night sky outside. West Ham and the neighbouring docks suffered badly in the bombing of 1940, but Thorne resisted entreaties that on account of his age and increasing infirmities he should be evacuated to the safety of the countryside, and remained among his constituents, sharing both their hardships and endeavours.

Though he continued to rise like clockwork at 7.30 each morning and retired promptly at 10.30 at night – proclaiming at his 87th birthday party that he fully intended to see-in his century – old age now suddenly began to hit him hard. In the autumn of 1943 he lost the circulation in both feet, and spent more than eight weeks bedridden. It was probably this loss of mobility that prompted his decision, taken a year later, that he would not stand again at the next general election. It was certainly one of the hardest decisions that he had ever taken, and his final appearance in the Commons, at the dissolution of Parliament on 15 June 1945, was charged with high emotion. He lived to see, and to celebrate, the return of the first majority Labour government, and was thrilled by the rendition of Jim Connell's *The Red Flag* sung by the Socialist MPs on taking their seats. It could not but have stirred within him a cavalcade of proud memories: of strikes and street fights, May Day rallies long past, of the smoke and fire of the retort houses, of congresses of the International, of hopes of a union for all general workers fulfilled, and of dreams of achieving Socialism still to be realised. He was made a Privy Councillor after the election, and on meeting Labour Party Chairman Harold Laski, after congratulating him on the achievement of power, told him that all that now mattered was the creation of the Welfare State and to see that, by doing so, 'the children get their chance'.[39]

The end, when it came, was mercifully swift. He died of a heart attack on 2 January 1946, and was buried in the East London Cemetery eight days later. The banner of the West Ham branch led the cortege, followed by hundreds of ordinary trade union members. A shrewd negotiator, courageous leader of men, and inspiring organiser, Thorne had brought unskilled men and women into the heart of the trade union movement, and had done as much as anyone to ensure that the New Unions would be Socialist in character, rather than Liberal or apolitical. When moving the union's motion on education at the TUC Congress in 1910, he had chosen to define himself 'as a revolutionary, class conscious, Trade Unionist and Social Democrat', and, within the context of the larger part of *My Life's Battles*, this is precisely how he should best be remembered. After all, he lived and died under the folds of the Red Flag. This book is one part of his lasting testament – the union that he founded is the other.

John Callow

NOTES

1. The dating of the foundation of the union is disputed. The union has always taken it to be Sunday 31 March, as this was the date Will Thorne recorded in his memoirs (see p66 of this edition of *My Life's Battles*). This has been disputed by Derek Matthews in *The London Gasworks: A Technical, Commercial and Labour History to 1914*, PhD Thesis (University of Hull, July 1981), p313. Matthews would seem to be correct, but does not give details to back up his claim. What, I would suggest, seems to have happened is that when, in 1925, Thorne came to write his autobiography, he used his old copies of *Justice* in order to aid his memory. As it happened,

Justice ran two separate stories about the founding of the union at Beckton. These were published in successive Sunday editions of the SDF journal, on 30 March 1889 and 6 April 1889, respectively. Both articles told, essentially, the same story but, if Thorne had only kept the second, it was an easy mistake to assume that the events recounted by the paper were from the previous weekend, rather than the fortnight before. See *Justice*, 30 March 1889, p3; 6 April 1889, p4.

2. See Matthews, *London Gasworks*, pp219-220, 225-226, 240, 251. As Matthews points out, while the gasworks accounted for fewer industrial deaths or injuries than work in the pits or on the railways: 'in 1898 gasworkers were 40 per cent more likely to die of bronchitis than other males; 33 per cent more likely to die of pneumonia; and 20 per cent more likely to die from influenza and cancer', op cit, p225.

3. W. Stephen Sanders, *Early Socialist Days*, The Hogarth Press, London 1927, p52. By way of coincidence, Stephen Sanders would also accompany Thorne on the TUC delegation to Russia, after the February Revolution of 1917. By that time he had left the SDF and was the effective head of the Fabian Society.

4. *Justice*, 30 March 1889, p3.

5. *Justice*, 27 July 1889, p2; 24 August 1889, p3.

6. Justice, 18 May 1889, p3.

7. *Justice*, 6 July 1889, p2.

8. *The Labour Elector*, 8 June 1889, p9.

9. Matthews, *London Gasworks*, pp338-339.

10. Matthews, *London Gasworks*, p380.

11. *The People's Press*, 22 March 1890, p5.

12. Anon, 'Bravo Barking!', *Justice*, 19 October 1889, p1.

13. *The People's Press*, 19 April 1890, p3.

14. Three members of the gasworkers' union were elected to Parliament at the general election of 1906: Will Thorne, James Parker, and J.R. Clynes. However, only Thorne was sponsored as the union's MP; Parker and Clynes were, instead, sponsored by the ILP. Curran, as a second union-sponsored MP, was returned for Jarrow

at a by-election in 1907, having been defeated in the constituency the year before.

15. H. Tracy (ed), *The British Labour Party. Its History, Growth, Policy and Leaders*, Vol. I, Caxton Publishing Company 1948, pp55-6.

16. P. Thompson, *Socialists, Liberals and Labour. The Struggle for London, 1885-1914*, Routledge & Kegan Paul, London 1967, p48.

17. C. Dukes, 'The Thorne I Knew', in GMWU, *Journal*, February 1946, Vol. 9 No.2, pp50-51.

18. See, for instance, Thorne, *My Life's Battles*, pp49, 138, 167.

19. E.P. Thompson, 'Homage to Tom Maguire' in A. Briggs & J. Saville (eds), *Essays in Labour History. In Memory of G.D.H. Cole*, Macmillan & Co. Ltd, London & New York 1960, pp276-316. For the counterview see Anon, 'The Great Gas Strike at Leeds', *The People's Press*, 5 July 1890, p6; Anon, 'The Great Strike at Leeds – Glorious Victory for the Union', *The People's Press*, 12 July 1890, pp6-7; and E. Aveling, 'How the Victory was Won', ibid, pp8-9. For their part, the Ironworkers at Millwall were in no doubt, when they met in July 1890, that Thorne was the 'Hero of the Leeds Lockout', see *The People's Press*, 19 July 1890, p10.

20. J.R. Clynes, 'Will Thorne', in H. Tracy (ed), *The British Labour Party. Its History, Growth, Policy and Leaders*, Caxton Publishing Company, London 1948, Vol. III, p236; J. Saville, 'Introduction' to W. Thorne, *My Life's Battles*, Lawrence & Wishart, London, 2nd edition 1989, ppxvi-xvii; and E.A. and G. Radice, *Will Thorne: Constructive Militant*, George Allen & Unwin Ltd, London 1974, p116.

21. G. Melia, *Will of Iron*, Longman, Harlow 1983.

22. E. George, *From Mill Boy to Minister: an Intimate Account of the Life of the Rt. Honourable J.R. Clynes MP*, T. Fisher Unwin, London 1918; and M. Bondfield, *A Life's Work*, Hutchinson & Co., London & New York, no date but 1949. See also *My Life's Battles*, p116.

23. Matthews, *London Gasworks*, p408.

24. *My Life's Battles*, p148.
25. *My Life's Battles*, pp218-29.
26. GMWU, *Journal*, November 1932, Vol. 9 No. 113.
27. K.D. Brown, *Labour and Unemployment, 1900-1914*, David & Charles, Newton Abbot 1971, pp73, 77, 83, 97, 99-100, 102-103, 133, 148, 150-152, 160, 171.
28. See, for instance, Radice, *Will Thorne*, pp72-3, 80, 101, 105-6, 109-110, 114, 116-9. The book's subtitle *Constructive Militant*, given the convulsions that the British Labour Movement was about to undergo in the late 1970s, effectively sets its tone, and also hints at the manner in which the union was then seeking to use – and re-deploy – history in the service of the present.
29. Matthews, *London Gasworks*, p392.
30. W. Thorne, 'To all Gasworkers', *The People's Press*, 22 March 1890, p9.
31. Matthews, *London Gasworks*, pp395 & 398.
32. Matthews, *London Gasworks*, p399.
33. Eleanor Marx to Samuel Gomperts, 23 February 1891; 11 June 1891: Eleanor Marx Papers, Microfilm ARCH01811, 8/1/103 & 8/1/105, International Institute of Social History, Amsterdam.
34. *The People's Press*, 12 April 1890, p10. For a recent, highly readable, study of Eleanor Marx – that does full justice to her role within the gasworkers' union, see R. Holmes, *Eleanor Marx. A Life*, Bloomsbury Publishing, London 2014.
35. *Justice*, 9 April 1898. The unpaginated edition, accessed by the present author, was located in Eleanor's archive at the International Institute of Social History, Amsterdam.
36. GMWU, *Journal*, January 1929, p207.
37. Will Thorne to Tom Mann, April 1936, framed photostat of an original letter, preserved at GMB National Office, Euston, London.
38. Thompson, *Socialists, Liberals and Labour*, p193.
39. H. Laski, 'Will Thorne', in GMWU, *Journal*, February 1946, Vol. 9 No.2, p52.

MY LIFE'S BATTLES

CHAPTER I

WORK AND PLAY

THE great East End of London, with its smoky skies, its slums, poverty, and all that is mean and ugly, has been my home for over forty years.

Here I still live among my people—dockers, labourers, casual workers in many queer and unpleasant trades. Our world is over-populated, our houses are small and poor, often a tightening of our belt strap takes the place of a meal. Towering factory chimneys are our sentinels, and the ships—tall ships, bright ships of many flags from far-off lands—our only inspiration.

I have often been asked why I am a Socialist, and why I persist in carrying on the fight to change this dull drab East End into a brighter place, and to make the people in it enjoy a freer and fuller life. My friends in the House of Commons, and many others I meet, say, with good intention perhaps, " We will always have slums and poverty." Perhaps as I tell you my story, which, with variations, is the story of hundreds of thousands of my East End neighbours and of millions of my brothers all over the country, you will begin to understand.

In a little four-roomed house, in the working-class district of Hockley, a suburb of Birmingham, I was born on an October morning in 1857. For some contrary reason the street was called Farm Street, but I have no memories of the free air of a farm during those early far-off days ; just the ugly houses and cobbly, neglected streets that were my only playground for a few short, very short, years.

Our house had no parlour, perhaps it would have been superfluous, for as both my father and mother worked in and around the brickfields there was little time for using parlours. Twelve hours' work was a short day then.

Their parents had been brickmakers before them. My mother was my father's second wife ; she married when very young, perhaps in the hope of escaping just such a home life as we had. A vain hope.

My father was a very good worker, and was fond of drink. The week ends would nearly always find him enjoying himself in this way, and he would add to his enjoyment by getting into a fight. Hardly a week would go by without a battle, and he earned the reputation of being somewhat of a terror. It was a common thing for him and his eldest son by his first wife to get into a four-cornered fight on these week-end sprees. They were his only diversion from work and sleep.

My father was a red-clay brickmaker, and every summer would travel to the brick works in different parts of Middlesex. When this summer work was over he would come back and sometimes work at the Saltley Gas Works as a stoker for the rest of the winter. This work was made precarious by the fact that the last man taken on in the winter should be the first dismissed when the " retorts " were shut down ; " priority work " it was called officially.

I was only seven years old when my father died in rather tragic circumstances in 1864. His death came about by a horse dealer hitting him a nasty blow in Lawley Street, Birmingham, one Sunday morning. He went to work the next day, but the blow had affected him so much that while at work he fell down in the muck and dirt and was taken to the Birmingham General Hospital, where he died the following Sunday.

The horse dealer was tried at the Warwick Assizes and was sentenced to nine months' imprisonment for manslaughter.

I remember my father's death quite well, although I was barely seven years old at the time, because the Sunday night that he died was the night that "Murphy's Riots" commenced in Carr's Lane, Birmingham. Protestants and Catholics came into conflict and hundreds of people were injured and taken to the hospital. I learnt after how the fight came about that caused my father's death. A publican that lived near our home had found one of the horse dealer's horses grazing in his fields. The publican asked my father to take it to the Pound, which he did, and the blow the horse dealer dealt my father was the revenge for assisting the publican.

My first job came when I was only a little over six years of age; it was turning a wheel for a rope and twine spinner at Rob's Rope Walk, Duddeston Mill Road, Vauxhall, Birmingham. I received 2s. 6d. per week, and worked from six in the morning until six at night, with a half-hour for breakfast and one hour for dinner.

There were no Acts of Parliament to govern the lives and working conditions of children then. On Saturday we worked from six in the morning until one o'clock midday, and when I was finished at the rope walk I had to go to my uncle, who kept a barber's shop, and help by lathering the customers' faces until about eleven o'clock at night, and then again on Sunday from eight o'clock until two in the afternoon, and for this work I was given 1s. a week. There were no laws governing the working hours or the sanitary conditions of barber shops, and I well remember the filthy and unsanitary conditions that I worked in.

It was at about this time I experienced my first strike. It was a brief one, over 6d. a week, and occurred when the spinner I worked for at the Rope Walk wanted to reduce my wages from 2s. 6d. per week to 2s. per week. I refused to accept this reduction and went on strike. But that strike was never settled and I never returned.

When my father died I was the eldest of four children. Our poverty compelled my mother to take any work she could get. She made a contract with a manufacturer of hooks and eyes to sew these small articles on thin cards. There were twelve hooks and twelve eyes to be sewn on each card, and the payment for this work was 1½d. per gross of cards, and my mother had to find her own needles and cotton. My elder sister used to help her, as well as looking after the two younger sisters. It was here I had intimate experience with sweated labour.

Like other boys I was anxious to get playing in the streets, and often I would put the younger children to bed very early, close the shutters and pull down the blinds to make them think it was dark. We were so poor at the time that my mother had made an application to the Birmingham Board of Guardians for Poor Law relief, and the Guardians had granted four loaves and 4s. per week. The bread was about as bad as it could possibly be, and it was my job to collect the relief every Wednesday from the Poor Law office about two miles from our home.

Those were days of hunger for all of us, especially on a Tuesday, when both bread and money had run out. In fact, Tuesday was nearly always a fast day ; sometimes I would take down the publican's shutters who was indirectly responsible for my father's death and he would give me a few coppers and sometimes a swede turnip, out of which I made a breakfast. I did not like the publican, but the hunger pain in my stomach drove likes and dislikes away.

My next job after the rope walk and the barber's shop was at a brick and tile works. At this place—Bond's Brick and Tile Works—I worked for my uncle. The place was three miles from our home, and each day a six-mile walk was added to the day's work of twelve hours. I think the Birmingham Football Ground is now on the site of these brick works.

My work was to carry away the bricks from my uncle. Each brickmaker had a shed to himself, and the bricks had to be laid out on a hot floor. In this way I had to handle from four to five hundred bricks a day. As my uncle made the bricks from two moulds I took them and laid them on this hot floor, and generally it was almost impossible to work with my boots and stockings on, so I did not wear any at all.

The work was heavy for a lad of my age. Each brick weighed about nine pounds, and in the course of a day I carried several tons of clay bricks. We usually started work at six in the morning, when I would pick up the bricks from the floor of the shed that had been dried from the previous day and night to make room for the fresh ones. Sometimes we would finish work at five o'clock, but it was generally later. It would depend upon the supply of clay from the clay-grinding mill.

We had to always make between four and five hundred bricks a day, even on Saturday, and so as to get work finished before three o'clock on Saturday afternoon I used to go home on the Friday nights, have some tea, pack my food, and then go to my uncle's house to sleep, so that we could be called about 3.30 on Saturday morning, get to work at four o'clock, get the task done and get off a little earlier than on the week days. There were no Saturday half-days like there are now. For this work I received 7s. a week. Later I had an advance of 1s. a week, making 8s. a week for doing a man's work.

After working with my uncle for a few months, I was put to look after one of the series of twenty-four fires that are attached to each kiln for the slow firing process. The bricks were put into the kiln, which was well sealed up at each end. The whole process of making in those days consisted of taking the clay after it had been dug up, and either "wielding" it in a "pug mill" or drawing it up an incline by a big chain. When the mass of clay had been thoroughly mixed the moulder would throw it into a mould and remove the surplus clay in the mould with a stick. The bricks were then taken from the mould and arranged on racks to dry in such a way as to allow a free passage of air around them. In about nine or ten days the bricks were ready for burning, and for this process they were formed into clamps or kilns having flues or cavities at the bottom for the insertion of the fuel. A fire was kindled in these cavities and gradually increased for the first three days and nights, after which it was kept at a uniform heat for several days and nights until the bricks were sufficiently burned. Much care was necessary in regulating the fire, because too much heat would vitrify the bricks and too little leave them soft and friable.

There are not so many bricks made by hand to-day as in those days ; they are now mostly machine made, and are less porous than the hand-made ones, and are more liable to crack in drying. They are smoother, however, and when carefully dried are stronger than the hand-made bricks.

Many nights I have had to sit up, putting coal on the slow fires during the burning process, and then in the day I would have to do my usual day's work. For the extra work I received 1s. per night.

I was discharged from this brick works one morning, after I had been up two consecutive nights looking after slow fires, when the head foreman caught me asleep at about four o'clock and a number of the fires almost burnt out. My uncle pleaded for me to be kept on, but I had committed an unforgivable sin, and the manager would have nothing but my dismissal.

After being out of work for two or three weeks I got a job in another brick works, which was further away from our home than the last job. As well as I can remember, it was a four-mile walk every night and morning, and I had to get up at four o'clock every morning to be at work at six. I worked the same number of hours as at the other brick works, but my new boss was a faster brickmaker than my uncle, and I had to travel backwards and forwards with each brick much faster to get the bricks away from the maker and on to the floor of the shed. If I kept him waiting a second or two he would give me a sharp tap on the head with a piece of wood that was used for levelling the clay at the top of the brick mould. The stick used was known as the " striker."

Because my new boss was a little faster we sometimes finished work at four o'clock, but I received no bigger wages—my share each week was still 8s.

There were two brothers, twins, companions of mine, working at this brick works, who used to live about the same distance from the works as I did, and we used to try and meet at the corner of Lester Street, Birmingham, at about 5.30 every morning. If we failed to meet after waiting a few minutes we used to place a stone in a certain position as a means of telling each other that we had gone on to work.

I remember at this time that several of the firm's horses were found dead. They had been stabbed, it was believed, by some one with a grievance against the firm. I think I was nine years of age at this time.

During the time that I was working at these brick works my mother got up at four o'clock every morning to give me my breakfast. I had to give up this job finally because my mother said that the work was too hard and the distance too long for me to walk every morning and night.

I remember her telling me that the 8s. a week would be missed ; some one would have to go short. But it was no use being slowly killed by such work as I was doing, and it was making me hump backed. It was not until I had been away from the work for several weeks that I was able to straighten myself out again.

My mother's rebellion against the way I was being worked is the rebellion of many mothers. It is the rebellion that I feel, and will continue to carry on. Just think for a moment. Here was I, a boy of nine years of age, that should have been in school, getting up in the cold of early morning, leaving home at about

4.30, walking four miles to work, and then, after a long twelve-hour day, walking back again, a fifteen-hour day by the time I got home, dead tired, barely able to eat my scanty tea and crawl into bed.

I know that it is not generally as bad as that nowadays, but there is still room for enormous improvement.

A few weeks' idleness and I was again on the job hunt. I found work with a master plumber and tinsmith, as a plumber's mate and general handyman. One of my tasks was to take the sheets of tin and lead after they had been cut into various lengths and hammer them with a wooden mallet into different shapes. Sometimes I used to go with the plumber to do work outside the shop, in private and public houses, fixing lead pipes. It was happier work than my previous tasks, but after nine months I left for some forgotten reason.

From plumbing I went to work for a lath splitter, where I had to saw logs into lath lengths, which were then split to certain thicknesses for use on walls and ceilings to take and hold the plaster. This work did not hold me long, and I was just about thirteen years of age when I ran into rather an unpleasant occupation. I started work for a firm that used to gather cow- and pig-hair from the butcher shops in and around Birmingham. It was a terribly dirty job, the hair smelt bad and was unclean to handle. We dressed and treated it, and the cow hair was used to mix with plaster, and the pig hair was sold, after washing and preparation, to hairdressers for making wigs. We would also buy hair from the barbers, which was used in the same way as the cow hair. One of the pleasanter parts of this work was calling at the barber shops with a horse and cart to buy and collect this hair.

At this time I was growing fast and taught myself to swim in the canal not far from our home. I learnt rapidly, and in a few months I could swim a mile with ease and make a fairly high dive. Often I would take a header from the top of the iron bars fixed to the top of the lock gates into the lock many feet below.

My fourteenth birthday happened about the time of the Franco-German War in 1871. I left the cow- and pig-hair trade and went to work at Abraham's metal rolling and ammunition works at Adderley Park Road, Birmingham. The first work that I was given to do here was pulling metal strips from the great rollers to the annealing furnaces, and filling a deep crucible with scrap metal that was melted and made into ingots.

The roar and the rattle, the steam and the heat of that inferno remains vivid in my memory, and many times I have dreamt of the place, waking up in a cold sweat of fear. I have other reminders of this brutalising work, for my hands to-day still show the scars I received when I was engaged on another job in this works : this was taking the annealed bars to the pickling tubs, where a strong vitriol solution was used for cleaning and pickling the metal. This biting acid would splash my hands and eat the flesh to the very bone, and only by washing my hands in milk was the excruciating pain eased and the effect of the vitriol killed. My clothes suffered badly from this solution : boots, trousers and shirts were attacked and eaten, and my shirt and trousers looked as though they had been the target for a dozen shot guns, so riddled with holes were they.

Often in later years, when I have been negotiating with different sets of employers, they have remarked at my detailed knowledge of workshop and factory conditions. I have shown an experience of their own works and methods that they themselves have not had. The getting of this knowledge was not through text-books or casual observation. In this ammunition factory I went from one process to another. After the pickling-tub work I was put to taking strips of metal out of the rollers as they came through ; from this I went to winding thin metal from another set of rollers ; and then to the brass rolling, where the golden yellow-looking sheets came out about the thickness of ordinary wrapping paper. Here I had to keep always on the alert, for the metal had to be kept straight and tight on the rollers, otherwise it became spoilt, and I received many a sharp knock or blow from my overman, Jack Groves. I soon learned to become a metal roller for strips and sheets, but the work was hard and killing, and it was gruesome to think that the metal we were handling was for making cartridge cases for both French and Germans to kill each other with.

Just as in the Great War, when munition work was being rushed through at high speed, so this firm was anxious to work every possible hour. Day shift men started at midnight on Sunday and worked right through until 5.30 on Monday evening. The night shift started at six o'clock and went through till six the next morning, coming back again at two o'clock the same Saturday and working again until nine o'clock at night.

For nine long months I saw little sunlight; the flowers and green things ablaze with glowing life were not for me, for I was on continuous night work. If I am sometimes blunt, and not altogether polite, it is such passages as this in my early working life that are reflecting themselves in any apparent bitterness that may be detected in my ways.

A strike occurred after I had been with this firm about six months—my second strike. It came about because the strip and metal rollers wanted an advance in pay. The firm were obdurate; they would grant nothing. The strike went on; attempts were made to get blacklegs and some were obtained. We dealt with them with vigour.

One chap returning home black from his work—our work and bread and butter—was stopped. We appealed to his manhood but without success. Nearby was a pond, and one of my mates, Bellamy by name, tried another method. He grabbed hold of the blackleg and threw him as though he were a bag of flour. The blackleg joined us and there were no more who were anxious to take our places.

Poor Bellamy got six months' imprisonment for throwing the blackleg into the pond, and his wife died while he was in prison. We did not forget either Bellamy or his wife, and all was done that should be in such circumstances to share the trouble and show appreciation of the action he had taken for us as well as himself.

During the strike we were somewhat at a loss what to do with our leisure time. It was strange, after either working or looking for work, to have any spare time, so some of the boys persuaded me to go home and get some things to pawn so that we could do a little drinking. Being young I was foolish enough to listen to them. I slipped home, took a new suit of clothes and boots, and some other things, and raised 15s. on them. We had a jolly time with the money, for we felt certain that, both on account of the shortage of labour and the urgent demand and big price being paid for the ammunition, that we would win the strike.

The firm were pressed for orders—Germans and French both wanted cartridges, and were paying well for them. The firm gave in and the advance in wages was granted. This was one of my earliest lessons in the law of supply and demand.

My last job at this works was working a set of rollers that broke down long thick strips of brass to thin metal pieces that were later drawn into wire. My pay for this was 18s. per week. The foreman took me off the work and gave the job to his brother, who received 22s. per week, and I was put back to another job.

The foreman and his brother had a quarrel and the brother left. I was asked to go back to my old job and do the same work for 18s. that the foreman's brother had been receiving 22s. for. I refused to do it and was told to draw what money was due to me and clear out.

I did not hesitate. I went, glad to be away from the grimy, noisy works, its heat and heavy labour. I always had hope that there were better jobs and better things in the future, and it was with no regret that I left what was to me a little hell on earth.

CHAPTER II

THERE are few rosy patches, if any, in the fight for bread in the lives of the manual labourer with little skill or education. Just long years of drudging work in the past and in the future. One can dream and hope, and if by chance God gives such a one imagination, it is more of a curse than a blessing. Much wisdom, it is said, brings much suffering, and while I may not be a wise man I have suffered much in mind and soul just thinking of to-morrow and to-morrow's morrow, as well as the physical sufferings and hunger that have been my lot and which are the lot of my people. . . .

The hell of the metal rolling works was behind me now; I was getting on to my sixteenth birthday, and I was labouring at Brown and Marshalls' waggon works, of Adderley Park, Birmingham.

I was always striving for something better throughout my life, and that is, perhaps, the reason why, in a little while, I was put to a semi-skilled engineer's work of tapping nuts and bolts. My wages were paid by the actual work I did—1½d. per gross for threading these nuts—and I had to work pretty rapidly to get through twelve gross of them in a day.

The work was not pleasant, for either a smelly oil or a soapsuds mixture was used on the tool to keep it cool when it was revolving its way through the hard iron or steel; it always left me in a mess at the end of the day. Soon I moved up a little more, and instead of tapping little machine nuts I was put to tapping the big coupling nuts used for coupling railway waggons and carriages together, and my wages went to 7s. a gross.

I found this work quite easy in comparison with some other jobs I had had. I found that I could turn out a gross of these nuts a day, but I came to the conclusion that if I worked at full speed and turned out a gross a day, which meant earning 7s. a day, my foreman would cut down the rate of payment. He did discover that I was not working at top speed and wanted to reduce the price to 5s. a gross. I would not accept this lower rate, and again I visited the paymaster and left. My third strike!

In passing I would like to say that just the fear I had of a fair rate for piecework being lowered when extra effort is made by a workman is the fear born of experience that still exists among all workmen.

One of the remarkable things about those times was, that no matter how hard men and boys worked, they were, whenever possible, always anxious to take part in sports, and so with myself. Just at this time I became keenly interested in boxing, running and walking. Perhaps my enthusiasm was sharpened by the fact that my mother's sister had married a professional boxer, " Mouse " Wilson, who was at the time one of the best known boxers in Birmingham. I remember him fighting with a man named Cunningham for over three hours. I forget the number of rounds, but they pounded away at each other in an open space, a crowd cheering as the dull thuds of the blows smacked out from ribs and arms. My uncle won the fight, adding, to my pride as well as his own, another victory to his already long list. Those who are acquainted with boxing history will remember " Mouse " Wilson.

Another thrilling fight of that time was fought with bare knuckles between Jimmy Ireland and Boxer Bradley. It was on a Monday night, my uncle, " Mouse " Wilson, called me about three in the morning, and we rode away in a trap with some other people and the two fighters for many miles. We travelled some distance because it was rumoured that the police had heard of the fight and were going to try and stop it.

We came to a big field, picked a suitable spot, fixed the ropes and fixed the stakes. The ring was ready and the men were at each other, fighting like demons. The fight lasted over an hour, both of the men were marked and covered with blood, and the victory went to Jimmy Ireland and youth, for he was the younger man.

A set of boxing gloves was soon after this in my possession, and my companions and myself started boxing and training at the street corner very nearly every night. Several of us became very handy with the gloves. We used to pummel each other, and arrange matches between ourselves, each contributing towards a stake, which, however, was rarely more than a shilling or two. Several times I won the stake money, but I often met defeat, especially against some of the bigger and heavier lads.

Another incident that occurred during this period stirred me to go in for walking and running. Near our home, the Vauxhall Gardens, a sports ground was situated, and a woman named Madame Angelo put up a record of walking a thousand miles in a thousand hours. She would walk a mile in the first quarter of an hour and then rest till the last quarter of an hour in the next hour, getting an hour and a half rest. She completed the thousand miles in the stipulated time. My training ground was a big square near where we lived. I would strip down to running drawers and shoes with my companions and go round and round the square both walking and running in " test races." At that time I was one of the best runners and walkers, and I was challenged to run without a stop from Birmingham to Coleshill, a distance of eight miles. I accepted the challenge and won the bet attached to it.

Another training place was a big block of buildings nearby ; three times around this block was figured as a mile. We used to strip down and have races of a mile and more for little sums of money. Often the police would interfere with our sport and threaten to arrest us, but in spite of the danger of the Law we continued our contests, so keen were we on the competition of it.

The first wave of cycling popularity caught us just after the height of our walking and running enthusiasm. The velocipede came into vogue. It was a light carriage, made of a simple framework resting on three wheels, and was propelled by the feet through two cranks attached to the axle. The wheels were made of solid iron, pneumatic and rubber tyres had not yet been manufactured. I bought one of these " boneshakers," as they were called, and soon learned to ride, but they were awkward to handle and lacked speed.

They never became very popular and were soon supplanted by the forerunner of the present bicycle, that was known as the " Penny-farthing." This was the two-wheeled bicycle that had a front wheel with the enormous diameter of about 52 inches and a tiny back wheel. The saddle was very high and a step was attached to the cycle to enable the rider to mount. I had some exciting times with this contraption in races with my companions on the Vauxhall Grounds, but even with the proficiency I attained I never had the courage to enter in any of the open races.

A brief spell of unemployment and I was back again among the noisy, rattling, clanging and banging of the metal-rolling mill. This time it was Everett's Works, in Adderley Street, Birmingham.

I took charge of a pair of metal rollers used for breaking down big copper ingots that were later rolled out into sheet copper. It was heavy, tiring work. I was soon put to another job—similar work, but not quite so hard—handling " wire metal," that is, long strips of copper that were fed into rollers again and again until the strips were in shape to be drawn into wire for making lightning conductors, telegraph wires, and a multitude of other purposes.

I seemed very unlucky about my wages, or people seemed to take advantage of me, for up to this time I had been receiving 22s. per week on the big rolls. I

was taken off them and put on another job, and the
man who was put in my place was given 24s. a week.
He was unable to do the work, so I was put back to the
job. I asked for the 24s. the other man had been
receiving, but the foreman would listen to no argument about the justice of the case I put up, and I ended
my career in the metal rolling trade with my fourth
strike.

There were exciting happenings in Birmingham during
my period of work at the rolling mills. The Navigation
Street riots were at their height. This street was at
the back of what is now New Street Railway Station.
It was a street of dilapidated houses and the haunt of a
very tough gang of roughs who were always looking for
trouble. They found it one Saturday night when they
ran foul of the police. It was a hot battle. One of the
policemen was killed with a brick and several others
were injured.

Most of the gang were arrested and tried at the Warwick Assizes by Justice Grantham. One of the men
was sentenced to death—his brother was working with
me at the time—and the rest of the gang were sentenced
to long terms of imprisonment, varying from seven to
fifteen years.

The action of the police resulted in the final clearing
up of the neighbourhood. It was a relief, especially for
the patrons of the Birmingham Theatre Royal, that
was adjacent to Navigation Street. This was a favourite
place for the gang to operate.

One of their games was to come along when the people
were lined up to go into the theatre. I was often in the
crowd, and just as the doors were open they would
leap-frog over the waiting crowd, run to the gallery and
take charge of all the best centre seats. Later they
would sell some of these seats, after keeping a number
for themselves. Up to the time of the riots neither the
police nor the theatre authorities were able to prevent
these raids.

Conditions were much better at the other music-halls,

where the proprietors were very strict about their patrons, who had to be decently dressed, and where no man was allowed in if he was not wearing a collar.

After my strike at the metal rolling mills I secured employment as a builder's labourer with a master builder named Johnny Garlick. The work I had to do for this man would have taxed the strength of a Samson. I would take a board and load it with bricks, lift this board on to my head, for which I had a pad, and then carry the load up the ladders to the bricklayers. Between times I would be excavating and mixing mortar. My wages were 4d. per hour. There has been a big improvement both in the method of working and the payment for this kind of work since those bad old days.

For only a few months could I stand this work, and I soon left Johnny Garlick to go back to work again in the brickfields. I got a job at Burk's, wheeling clay for my cousin, Jim Thorne. He was one of the fastest brick-makers in Birmingham and the champion cribbage player in the district.

I found working with a champion brickmaker a hard life. In addition to wheeling the clay, I had to operate the press used for pressing the bricks and putting a smooth surface on them. My wages at this time came to 3s. 6d. per day. The brickmakers were paid piece-work, at so much per thousand, or so much per dozen in the case of fancy bricks. Out of his wages the brick-maker had to pay his clay wheeler and the boy engaged in carrying the bricks away from the moulding table.

The manager wanted to reduce the price for making bricks, and after having a talk with the manager my cousin asked me what I thought about the matter. He said that if he accepted the lower rates of payment for making he would have to reduce my wages. My reply was brief. I told him that I would not take a penny less than I was then receiving, and the end of the dis-cussion was that we both of us left the works, with me putting the fifth mark on my strike register!

That was in 1875, when I was just eighteen years of
age, and also the time of my mother's second marriage
to a man named George Thompson, a carpenter and
joiner. He was a double-handed drinker. I thought
that my mother would have been more careful in her
selection of a second husband, after her first experience,
but she made a worse choice, for the second one was
even a heavier drinker than my father. He had a
violent temper and was very quarrelsome. It was
through this stepfather and his behaviour that I left
home to go on the " tramp," and the last I heard of
him was that he died in the poorhouse.

Tramping is not as romantic as it is supposed to be ;
at least, it was not in those days, although we got a
certain amount of fun out of our experiences.

I found a companion in the same plight as myself, and
with only a few coppers in our pockets we started out.
Mile after mile we went along the country roads, in-
quiring in villages and towns for work as we went, but
we had no luck.

At Burton we slept in a common lodging-house for
4d. a night. It was a very rough place. Most of the
lodgers were navvies, and the language they used in
their arguments and quarrels would make the famous
" blue " talk of Billingsgate sound like refined and
cultured conversation.

At the lodging-house we got into conversation with
an old navvy. He told us we could get work at what
was known as the Burton and Derby Railway, then
under construction.

In the morning we started out for the railway cutting
to interview the foreman ganger. Father Fairbanks, as
he was called, was the contractor, and we started work
for him at 2s. 6d. per day. A new shovel was supplied
to us, for which we had to pay 2s. 6d. out of the first
week's earnings.

My companion was not used to this class of work, and
the first day of handling the shovel brought big blisters
up on his hands, so he gave it up. I had, however, used

shovels so much that it did not affect me. The shovel and I were old friends, but the work was hard and heavy. I had to fill so many waggons of muck a day. As a rule two men worked together filling a waggon, and if they filled more than the given number fixed as a day's work they received a little extra pay.

I held this job down for some time, lodging at one of the huts near to the work. It was kept by a very respectable navvy ganger who was working on the same job as myself. There were several of the other navvies staying at the same place. At five o'clock every morning we got up, had a jolly good breakfast and started work at six. The food was both good and plentiful and we were charged 12s. a week for board and lodgings. This did not leave me much out of my earnings of 15s. per week. Some of the other navvies, of course, earned more than 15s. There was a farmhouse near the hut where we could buy milk for 2d. per quart, and the navvies, including myself, were very good customers of this farm.

The man who ran the hut, being a navvy himself and knowing the thirst-provoking character of the work, used to get in barrels of beer that he retailed to us at 4d. per quart. He had some other beer, which was not so strong, that he sold at 2d. per quart. This was my favourite drink because of its cheapness.

The inclusion from time to time of pheasants, partridges and rabbits in our menu was somewhat of a mystery to me until I noticed that several of the navvies had lurcher dogs—fast animals, built on the lines of a greyhound. I knew they were good game-getters, and that game was plentiful in nearby fields, but I never knew when the poaching was done. I was very inquisitive and watched, and I soon noticed that several navvies were missing from the hut at night. I inquired and found that in a shed near by a lot of rabbit traps and nets were kept, and these were used both by the boss and his lodgers to go poaching with at night.

Later on I often went on these poaching parties and

enjoyed the sport.   One Saturday morning, very early, we were returning home along one of the roads with a heavy bag of game when we noticed a policeman behind us.   He was obviously following us, so we put our best leg forward and ran for home.   Only after doubling across some fields and dodging around some buildings did we get safely to the hut.

This was not the end of the chase, however, for the next day a plain-clothes policeman came to the railway cutting to try and find the poachers, but he did not discover the men who had eluded the policeman the day before.   If he had we should certainly have been sent to prison, for in those times the local magistrates were nearly all squires, who looked on poaching as a terrible offence, and one that should be punished with nothing less than three months " hard," without the option of a fine.

After navvying for a little time I saved up enough money to pay my railway fare back to Birmingham.   I could get no work when I arrived back until I came on a job at a place called California, about seven miles out from the town.   There I had to take bricks through a tunnel from a yard to the edge of a canal, where they were loaded on barges and taken to different parts of the country.

The pay there was better than at my last two jobs, for I received 5d. per hour.   The first week I could not find any lodgings in or near California, so I walked seven miles each morning and evening from Birmingham. This made it necessary for me to leave home at four o'clock in the morning, and I never returned until about eight o'clock at night.

If you can imagine how I felt after doing a fourteen-mile walk and a hard day's work handling heavy bricks every day you can begin to realise what general working conditions were like in those days before the workers had trade unions strong enough to protect their interests.

Most of the bad conditions were certainly due to the

ignorance of the men and their boastfulness; the navvies, in particular, being very proud of themselves, and liking to be called " Thick Leg." They were " Thick Leg Jack " or " Thick Leg Tom," and the bigger the calves of their legs were the prouder they were to show them beneath their short, tied-up trousers. I have known them to wrap pieces of calico around their calves to make them bulge and give them a " Thick-legged " appearance.

I managed, after a week or two, to find lodgings near my work with two old people who had been " monkey-boat " workers on the canal. The " monkey-boats " were the very narrow canal boats that were dragged up and down the canal by horses.

These people were both about sixty years of age. The woman used to smoke a clay pipe, and they both used to get very drunk and fight each other several times during the week. I could not put up with their brawl-ing, and after a few weeks I packed up and cleared out and finished with navvying for good.

Coming back to Birmingham I fell in with my old companions, who were working at the gas works. Their amusement at this time was pigeon flying and dog and cock fighting. On Saturday nights we would go to a public-house and make bets on the contests that would be held on the next Sunday morning.

The contests were held in the following way. Two or three of us would be sent to a place some distance away, such as Warwick or Walsall, taking several pigeons and a stop-watch with us. At a certain time we would release a pigeon, and then the others, at two-minute intervals, according to the instructions we had been given.

The official timekeeper was stationed at the public-house, and as the pigeons arrived the owners had to catch them and show them to the timekeeper, who would make sure that the bird was the one it was sup-posed to be. To assist in this each pigeon had some sort of mark on it. Quite a lot of money changed hands over these races, and a real keen interest was taken in the breeding of the birds.

The dog fights were very brutal; I did not like to see them. It is bad enough when two dogs get to fighting in the street, but these dogs were specially-trained prizefighters. The fights would take place in a yard, the owners backing their dogs for substantial sums of money. As soon as the dogs were let off their leashes they would fly for each other's throat, and I often saw a dog with its throat torn open. The grim battles would go on, with growling and snapping, until one or both the dogs were completely exhausted. The referee would decide which was the winner, just as if it was a boxing match.

Cock fighting was just as brutal as the dog fighting. Special prize cocks were kept for the purpose. When they were fighting they would be armed with sharpened steel spurs attached to their feet. The fights would go on until the birds were exhausted. I have seen a cock fight last for over thirty minutes. Just as with the dog fights, the referee would give a decision as to which bird had won.

Often the decisions would lead to fights between the owners of the birds and the spectators on account of the money involved both as stake money and in side bets.

Among the spectators there was often a very good type of man known as the " travelling navvy." These chaps were always travelling the country taking navvy work wherever it offered. They have helped to do the rough, hard work of many of our biggest public and private enterprises.

It was the custom of a navvy working on a job always to see that these " travellers " had a shilling or two if they could not obtain work; a " bob a nob " was the regular collection. They were a picturesque-looking lot of men, with their knee breeches and watertight boots. They were good-hearted, and when they had money they spent it quickly, dressing and living well.

I am sure that the days that I spent in the open air, working as a navvy, living with these big-hearted, care-free men, and absorbing their conversation, had much to do with my future. They were an independent type, with the spark of rebellion glowing bright within them. Living and working with them, and then leaving navvy-ing to become unemployed for some time, did not give rise at the time to any definite thoughts in my mind. That came later. But it was at the time I was with these big, free-hearted men that my sub-conscious mind was at work.

The cold hand of winter was across the land, and chill blasts were not conducive to philosophical thinking. It was work, work, and the ever-pressing need for bread that I was thinking about.

I turned again to the gas works at Saltley and obtained the means of earning my bread by wheeling away coke from a gang of stokers in the retort house.

The work was hot and very hard. As the coke was drawn from the retort on to the ground we threw pails of water on it, and the heat, both from the ovens and the clouds of steam that would rise from the drenched coke, was terrific.

Once cooled, the coke had to be wheeled away and pitched on to a big heap. For this we used a great six-pronged fork. It was gruelling work. The place was running night and day. We worked a twelve-hour night for two weeks, and then a twelve-hour day for the next two weeks. The change-over from day work to night work was dreadful. Ordinarily the work was agonising—twelve hours a day in heat and steam, and exposed to draughts ; bending and straining the back and arms, taxing the muscles until they became numb— but the change-over multiplied all this.

We would start work at six o'clock on a Sunday morning, the last day in a two-week shift, and work the twenty-four hours right through until six o'clock on Monday morning. Every extra hour after the first twelve seemed like a month, and when these twenty-four-hour stretches came to an end I used to be absolutely exhausted in body and mind.

It would be well into the middle of the next week before I began to feel normal again, after these long stretches of inhuman labour.

About February of each year some of the retort houses would be shut down ; the days would be growing longer and not so much gas would be consumed as in the winter. This meant unemployment for many. As a junior and a late-comer to the works I was one of the first to go.

I was not sorry, and spent a happy summer excavating for my old boss, Johnny Garlick, who was starting a new brickfield. My job was fairly pleasant—cutting away the top surface of the soil so that we could get at the clay. This finished, I had a turn at wheeling clay for the brickmaker. I spent the summer on this job and returned to the gas works at Saltley in November.

As a leader of men and strikes I made a beginning shortly after my return to the gas works. From those days, when there were no trade unions for the semi- and unskilled workers, until 1924, with its great combinations of hundreds of thousands of workers under one democratic control, I have fought many fights, strikes, lockouts and agitations to secure just a little more bread, a little more comfort. These battles have been my daily work. " There are too many strikes and labour troubles," is the cry that goes up from time to time, but always from people who know little or nothing of the everyday lives of the workers.

Listen to the conditions that I and my mates worked under at this gas works, and then ask yourself whether you would have been content to work under such conditions without complaint.

I am back at the gas works wheeling coal to the stokers ; a week or two passes, and I am, by luck or circumstances, a fully-fledged stoker, drawing and charging retorts and looking after the fires, and my wages are 5s. per day.

The retort houses are exceedingly hot, for both behind and in front of the stoker are the burning eyes of
the furnaces ; amidst the roaring of the heat-hungry
retorts a breeze as of hell fans me. This is my job ;
these are my conditions.

A new furnace had been installed. It was the inven-
tion of a German, and was like a great mouth organ.
The hot air used to pass through the many passages
and generate a terrific heat, that would carbonise about
4 cwt. of coal in about four hours. This was a saving
of at least two hours on the old retorts. The new
furnace made working conditions even more unbearable
than the old one. It was almost impossible to stand for
long on the floor in front of it.

The working day consisted of twelve hours, and
every day in the week was worked. I was willing to
work, but I wanted human conditions to work under.
The terrible twenty-four-hour shifts at the time of the
change-over could not be altered ; they were the result
of Sunday work. The remedy was the abolition of
Sunday work. I called a meeting of the stokers in the
mess-room. They came fearing the wrath of their
employer, lest he should hear of their conduct ; there
was little revolt in them. I talked to them, I appealed
to them ; I suggested that a deputation should go to
see the general engineer—a Mr. Hack, a man with a
very violent temper—and ask for the abolition of
Sunday work. My fellow-workers turned me down.
They said that it was impossible to abolish Sunday
work in the retort house, because it would shorten the
lives of the retorts ; they argued that, if the fires were
banked up on Sunday morning and not used again until
Sunday night, the retorts would begin to crack.

Labour leaders can testify that often their hardest
work is not in fighting the employers, but in driving the
fear out of their own men. They will tell you, also, that
their hardest kicks and greatest abuse come from those
they are trying to help and serve.

So it was with me. They put up all sorts of arguments

against my proposal, but I stuck to them. " It seems to me," I said, " that you think more about the lives of the retorts than you do about your own lives." This remark had the right effect. They plucked up courage, and said they would form a deputation if I would be spokesman. I agreed.

We first saw the resident engineer, Mr. Schoolbred. I explained to him the difficult tasks we had to perform. I told him how the twenty-four-hour " change-over " shifts, when we were changing from day to night work, or *vice versa*, were paralysing our strength and sapping our energy, and certainly shortening our lives.

He listened to me, and then produced the same arguments that my companions had used in the mess-room. He was firmly of the opinion that the reform I wanted could not be achieved. I stood firm. He said he would have to consult the chief engineer. I demanded that he should do so as speedily as possible, for by this time I had the men with me ; their dulled intelligence had at last seen the justice of the case I had put up, and it had dawned upon them that they held the power to compel the reform to be made. They were ready to down tools and go on strike. I counselled patience while the meeting was arranged with the violent-tempered chief engineer.

A few days passed ; the deputation was to meet the chief in one of the long mess-rooms, and I was to be spokesman. I had no fear. I launched out at him with the same statements that I had made to the men and to the resident engineer. I expressed my views and those of the men in simple, strong language. I emphasised the points about working twelve hours a day for seven days a week, and showed him that this gave the men no opportunity to have a Sunday off to meet relatives, who may be living a little way off ; that none of us were able to go to church or chapel. I ended with the warning that, if the system he was working us by was continued, it would drive us to become " materialists " and other sinister persons.

He raved up and down the mess-room, threatening us, and refusing to consider our demand. If we did not like the place and the work, we could clear out. In reply to this, I told him that it would not only be the deputation that would clear out, but that all the men in the works would leave in a body. He saw that we were in earnest and determined to make a stand, so he altered his tone and promised to give the matter serious consideration.

The gas works was run by the Birmingham Corporation ; the then Mayor was the late Right Hon. Joseph Chamberlain. We were promised that the whole matter would be laid before the Gas Committee. We waited.

The ignorance of the Mayor and his committee of working conditions was shown when he visited the works, accompanied by the chairman and members of the Gas Committee. When they passed through the retort house, we had just finished drawing and charging a set of retorts, and were having a " breather."

I heard Chamberlain ask the foreman why we were " fooling about and sitting down " ! As a matter of fact the sweat was rolling off us at the time, and our muscles were aching from the hot fast work of drawing and recharging the retorts.

Victory was the result of this, my first effort to improve the conditions of the gas workers. Two weeks after the interview with the chief engineer the matter was laid before the Gas Committee, but we did not know their decision until the chief engineer called a deputation of the men to meet him in the mess-room.

My heart throbbed with excitement as we waited for him to speak, and I exulted when he announced : " The Gas Committee has decided to do away with Sunday work from 6 a.m. to 6 p.m. No payment will be made for Sunday."

This meant a reduction of 5s. per week. We started to work under the new system two weeks after the eventful victory meeting in the mess-room.

The fruits of our victory at the Saltley works were shared by the workers at the other two corporation works—at Windsor Street and Adderley Street—where the new system was also put into operation.

I was greatly encouraged with the success of my agitation. When I first took it into my head to seek the abolition of Sunday work, I feared that my pals might not stand behind me ; there were no trade unions and no finances to back up the workers or to watch their interests. Congratulations came to me from all who had benefited by my action, but I did not lose my head, for I realised that the victory we had won was, after all, not the full achievement of the Social Revolution.

I learnt during this dispute more than anything else the absolute necessity for the combination of workers in trade unions if there was to be any improvement in their wages and working conditions. I therefore started an agitation with a view to getting the gas workers to form a union. My immediate reason was to get a reduction in the working hours, for I knew that, with such a reduction, more men would be employed, our labour would become more valuable, and our economic and industrial strength greater.

I had to deal with very ignorant men. I could make no headway. I told them on one occasion that they did not have the brains of a rabbit. I must admit that I myself was not well educated, and I did not know a great deal about the political and industrial Labour Movement, but the men lacked something else beside brains—they had no courage. They were, of course, not to be blamed. The long hours of tiring work, and the home lives they endured, robbed their brains and bodies alike of any chance to develop the natural characteristics of a normal man.

I told some of my mates that I would have to be very careful in attempting to organise and form a union among them, for I knew full well that the weapon of victimisation, the " sack," would be used against me if I were found out by the " heads." The chief engineer was nursing a grievance against me for my success in securing the abolition of Sunday work. It had meant a small increase in the cost of production of gas, and he, like all other managers, wanted costs down and profits up. The ratepayers benefited by the profits, and more was thought of them than of the lives of the workers in a public utility firm—those who did the heavy and arduous work of it.

One day, while I was sitting down writing, I received an order that I had to go to work in what we called the " purifiers." This meant a reduction in pay, and was the means chosen by the chief engineer of hitting back at me over the Sunday work business. There was no other reason for the change, for I had lost no time nor had I neglected my work at the retorts.

The chief, at this time, was anxious to bring about economies wherever possible, perhaps to counterbalance the cost of not working on Sunday. He introduced a new system of conveying coal into the retort houses. This did away with the coal wheelers, because the coal was thrown direct from the railway trucks into the retort house. This system saved wages, but made exceedingly hard work for the stokers, who, instead of having the coal wheeled to them, had to take it direct from the new chutes.

The retorts held about 3 cwt. of coal, and were about eighteen feet long. At a given signal the stokers on both ends of the retort would begin to shovel the coal in. The first shovelfulls had to go half-way down the retort, and a considerable amount of force was needed to do the work.

A new method of loading the retorts was introduced ; it was called " scoop work." The scoop was about nine feet long and had a long handle attached to it. The scoops held about 1 cwt. of coal, and three men worked in a gang operating them—one man to guide the scoop, and two in front to lift it up on to a ledge into which it fitted. When this was done the whole scoop would be lifted up and the contents slung into the retort.

The introduction of this work would have led to a

strike, but again there was no union to support the men in demanding an adjustment of their work. I tried again to form a union. I saw that the scoop work meant less rest for the men and multiplied work, not alone because more coal had to be fed into the retorts, but because a correspondingly greater amount of coke had to be wheeled away—bigger tasks were allotted to the men. There was a lot of discontent among the men, but they did not have the grit to combine and use their collective power to try and get the work reduced.

My patience was sorely tried by their apathy, and I almost gave up in despair. What I was after was a reduction of hours by the abolition of the twelve-hour day, and the establishment of the eight-hour working day. It was not to be, however, and it was not until much more fighting, and after the union was formed, that this great reform was secured.

Odd memories come to me of those times. There was a fine fellow, a navvy who worked on the purifiers, known as the " Rat Catcher." I used to go with this companion to a farmhouse not far from where we were living. Going around by the pig-styes, he would let a ferret loose that he used to carry inside his shirt. The ferret would drive the rats from their holes and they would be caught in a net. A great number of rats would be caught in this way. The " Rat Catcher " sold them to the owners of the prize-fighting dogs, that I have already mentioned, who would throw them into a pit. The dogs would then be let loose in the pit, and the dog that killed the most rats would win a money prize for its owner. This was a brutal and disgusting form of sport, to my mind, and I never took much interest in it.

My life was full of interest; the conditions of the workers and how to improve them occupied my mind quite a lot. I was also courting the girl who later became my wife. She was the daughter of Mr. Jack Hallam, a well-educated, clever man, a Radical in politics, and I learnt much from him about political economy.   His wife was a bonny woman, with a big, kind heart.

While courting I often visited their house.   They made me welcome and I had many a good meal with them.

Mr. Hallam worked at the Saltley Gas Works in the winter and in the brickfields in the summer.   Later on he became the foreman at one of the retorts at the gas works.   He had a big family of boys and girls—a jolly crowd.   When I look now at my eldest daughter, I see the image of her mother.

Finally, on February 9th, 1879, when I was twenty-two years of age, I tired of living a single life in lodgings and I married Miss Hallam after a courtship that had lasted for sixteen years.   I have the marriage lines in front of me as I write.   I see that neither of us could write, for both of us made our " mark " on the marriage certificate.

It was a Monday morning when we got married.   I had been working all night, but we went along to St. Anne's Church, in the parish of Aston, in the county of Warwick, and did the deed.   I went to work again that evening.   That was our honeymoon !   But I have jumped ahead of my story.

The first election campaign I remember was when the three Liberals, Joseph Chamberlain, John Bright and a Mr. Muntz, ran in Birmingham with a Mr. Calthorpe and Captain Burnaby as Tory opponents.

The Liberal organisation was very good ;   in some parts of the division the electors were advised to vote for Chamberlain and Bright, in another for Chamberlain and Muntz, and in others for Bright and Muntz. This strategy was successful, for all three got elected.

There have been big improvements in voting arrangements since then.   Schools were not used as polling booths, but hastily-constructed wooden sheds, placed at street corners.   Considerable excitement took place outside these booths ;   questionable methods were adopted ;   and there was many a row and fight.

Some little time after the election Major Bond became the Chief of Police of Birmingham. He was a strong disciplinarian. Before his election to this position he made the ridiculous declaration that he would make the city so honest that he would be able to hang his watch and chain on a lamp post in the roughest and poorest part of the town and be able to find it there twenty-four hours later. He never tried the experiment ! He did not know the people of Birmingham.

Much has been said and written about the drinking habits of the poor people of those days. The stories are highly exaggerated. We did have our jollifications, but they were never so bad as people make out. In the way of drinking we had a custom at the gas works that when a coke wheeler was promoted to the position of stoker, which meant an increase of 1s. per day in his wages, he had to pay his " footing." This would be done by him giving a sum of 10s. to 15s., to which we would all add 1s. When the money was collected we would arrange to meet at a public-house and have a spree. Nobody would get very intoxicated, though we would all be jolly, singing songs and congratulating the stoker on his promotion.

Beer was not allowed inside the works, except with the workers' meals that were brought by their wives or children at the meal times. We evaded this prohibition at nights, after the foreman had gone away, and when we had a spell between charging and drawing the retorts one of us would slip out and bring back a can or two of beer. No blame could be placed against the gas workers for this when it is realised how hot, hard and heavy the work is—work of such a nature that would not permit the men to drink tea, cocoa or water and remain well. The management realised this after a time and allowed each man a half-pint of oatmeal a day, but it was not as thirst-quenching as beer.

The gas workers were a jolly, comradely lot of men, but sometimes we had our disagreements. I remember one night when I was charging the retorts, my mate on the opposite end slacked down, making my work much harder. After we had finished I went around and told him about it. His contribution to the argument was to give me a punch in the mouth.

To fight in the works meant getting the " sack," so I challenged him to fight the matter out later. Four days later we met to settle our differences and to fight for a stake of 10s. I thought, even though my opponent was bigger than myself, that my earlier boxing experience would pull me through the battle, but I soon found out that he was also a good boxer.

We pulled off our shirts to fight, and got at it with the bare fists. There was little fancy work ; he played on my ribs with rapid and heavy punches, and I contented myself with making his face my target. In the fifth round I injured my thumb, and as I dropped my guard I collected two lightning blows on my eyes. I had to give in and so lost the fight and the 10s. stake money. The fight kept us both away from work for a couple of days, as a result of the punishment we handed each other, and I was not anxious to exhibit my " two lovely black eyes."

This fight was a tame affair to one I got mixed up in at the " Duke of Edinburgh," a public-house near where I lived. The place at that time was very dilapidated ; later on the owner of it won £10,000 on the Doncaster St. Leger and rebuilt the place and a row of houses as well.

The fight happened when I was playing in a four-handed game of cribbage. My partner was an old boxer and he noticed that one of the other players was cheating, and gave him a stinging punch. In a minute glasses, bottles and tables were flying about the place, blood was flowing, while kicks and punches were being delivered unmercifully. The police, luckily, were not about, and the only things we suffered were the cuts, scratches and soreness from the brawl.

This drinking and fighting should not be magnified or misjudged. We were healthy, normal human beings, fond of fair play ; we had little amusement and little opportunity to enjoy the better things of life. If these fights sometimes took place, it was no fault of ours, but rather of the system of society we lived under—a system that made us work long hours of brutalising toil for little money ; a system that had no care as to the slums we slept in, the food we ate, or the education we received or tried to give our children. We were poor, ignorant victims of the growing machine of industrialism, and the progress we have made since those days has not been because of the Christian hearts of the more fortunate ones above us, but because of our innate love of freedom that has been developed in the incidental battles for bread.

In the days I write of now working-class history was gestating in the womb of time. Great days were ahead, days of fighting and building, for it was in the few eventful years that were to follow that the foundation stones of the present great new Trade Union Movement and Labour Party were laid.

I was always in the forefront of workshop and factory agitations. My main battle ground was, however, in the gas works in which I was employed, whether Birmingham or London. The student of industrial history and social science may ask why, and the only reason that I am able to give—a sufficient one in my opinion—is that the system we lived under at that time, the poverty and hardships the workers had to endure— the hard work and long hours, and the tender age at which we were thrown into the industrial battle field— made us rebels.

It made me one at an early age, for I was only fifteen, working at the metal-rolling mills, when I swore that I would do everything in my power to help prevent other children going through the same hardships, misery, and suffering that I had to go through.

I did not understand the methods of production ; I had no opportunity, and very few workmen were wiser than I on the subject. The economic and industrial system of capitalism, in which production was for the purpose of profits, and not for use, was a mystery of which we knew nothing. There were few books accessible to the workers, and working-class propaganda had hardly started. Later in my life I read such books as Karl Marx's "Capital," "European Society," by Sketchley; Frederick Engel's "Socialism: Utopian and Scientific," and other books by Marx, Engels, Hyndman, Bellamy, Blatchford, Robert Owen, Richard Green, and many others. They helped me to understand the problems I was faced with. What helped me more than the books even was the personal contact I had with great thinkers and working-class leaders like Karl Liebnecht, Herr Bebel and Singer, Dr. Adler, and Frederick Engels, of Germany; Paul Lefarge and the wonderful Jean Jaures, of France. One of the greatest orators this country ever heard, Dr. Aveling, gave me much help, and Eleanore Marx-Aveling, Karl Marx's third daughter, used to assist me to improve my reading and handwriting, which was very bad at the time.

The great William Morris and H. M. Hyndman, with whom I came in contact quite a lot, had a big influence on me. As my story continues I will tell of my associations with Charles Bradlaugh, Mrs. Annie Besant, Keir Hardie, Pete Curran, and of the times when I met King Edward, Lord Kitchener, Lenin, and many other great people.

The Birmingham Corporation, which owned and controlled the gas works, were always anxious to effect savings in wages. To this end they introduced a machine for drawing and charging the retorts. It was operated by compressed air, and was known as the "iron man."

I was put to work with this machine. One machine was used on either side of the retorts. Four of the stokers worked with the machines, charging the retorts with coal and drawing off the coke, instead of using the old hand rakes and shovels.

The machines made the work heavier for the men.

In fact, so hard and rapid was the work that we often had no time to eat our food between charges. The machine was constantly breaking down, and this would put us behind with the work, for, breakdown or no, we had to do our same number of charges, and in trying to catch up with the work after one of these stoppages we had a heartbreaking task. Sometimes we could not catch up, and there would be trouble with the Welsh foreman, whom nobody liked.

When summer came, this foreman was instructed to get the work done with two men less, and so I and a companion were left to do the work of four men on one machine, and two men on the other side of the retorts to do the work on another machine. It was an almost impossible task. For a few days we complained, but could not get our grievance rectified. Finally we had a meeting, and decided to refuse to carry on any longer. We declared a strike, got our pay, and marched out of the works.

After we had left, the machines were shut down for a time, and when they were restarted the work was made easier and more satisfactory to the men who, while not standing by us, had benefited by our strike. This often happens, for there are lots of workers too cowardly to stand by their comrades in fighting for their rights, but who are always prepared to accept any advantage won by them.

Three of us who had gone on strike obtained work at a drainage scheme near Birmingham, at 5*d*. per hour. While we were on this job we had several talks about going down to London.

CHAPTER III

I HAD always wanted to go to London, and my desire to go to the biggest city in the world was stimulated by letters from an old workmate at the Saltley works, who was now working at the Old Kent Road Gas Works, in London. This gas works was owned by the South Metropolitan Gas Company, and managed by the late George Livesey, who was a son of the great temperance reformer. The son was also a temperance man, and I shall have more to say about him when I come to deal with the big strike that took place with this company in 1889.

The letters from my friend—his name was Walter Evans—continued to come to me. He gave glowing reports about what was going on in London. His descriptions of the costermongers' market in East Street, Walworth, were interesting and graphic pictures of the life in those parts, especially on Saturday nights.

This friend also wrote about the scenes in Petticoat Lane and "Club Row"; about the way some Jews used to swindle and cheat people by selling shoddy goods, and the way they used to pretend to sell three half-crowns for $1\frac{1}{2}d$. by putting them into a purse before the people's eyes and telling them not to open the purse before they got home. Many people were foolish enough to be gulled by this trick. I have seen the same people selling painted sparrows as canaries, and doing other dishonest tricks.

I finally decided to go to London in November, 1881. With two friends I started out to walk the journey, filled with the hope that we would be able to obtain employment, when we got there, with the kind assistance of my friend Walter Evans.

We had little money when we started, not enough to pay for our food and lodgings each night until we arrived in London. Some days we walked as much as twenty miles, and other days less.

Our money was gone at the end of the third day, and we had to rely on the kindness of people along the road and in the towns we passed to get food and lodgings.

For two nights we slept out—once under a haystack, and once in an old farm shed. Arriving at St. Albans, I met an old friend with whom I had worked at Birmingham. I told him how we were fixed—footsore and hungry, and still many miles from the Old Kent Road Gas Works, where we hoped to obtain employment.

This friend was a friend indeed. He gave us a good meal, got us a bed, and the next morning we took the train into London.

On arrival in London we tried to find out where my friend Walter Evans lived, but we were unsuccessful. Our money was all gone, so there was nothing for us to do but to walk around until late at night, and then try to find some place to sleep. We found an old building and slept in it that night. The next day, Sunday, late in the afternoon, we got to the Old Kent Road Gas Works, and applied for work.

To my great surprise the man we had been looking for was working at the time. He spoke to the foreman and I was given a job, but my two friends were not taken on.

My first job at this gas works was pulling coke barrows from the stokers, full of red-hot coke. The barrows we used were heavy two-wheeled iron ones, and the coke had to be drawn out of the retort house into the open yard, where I had to throw water on the coke and stack it up into a heap.

The long walk from Birmingham, with little sleep or food, and then this hard work, had tired me out, so much so that I fell asleep several times between pulling the loads out.

After my first night's work, I obtained lodgings in the Prince of Wales' Road, just off the Old Kent Road.

Dark winter days of fog and cold were drawing in, more men were wanted at the works, and the two friends I had walked to London with were given work with us. We at the works had been keeping them going until this time, and it was quite a relief when this drain on our slender wages was ended.

George Livesey, the chairman of the company, was a very strict employer. As I have already mentioned, he was a strong advocate and worker in the cause of temperance, and he would allow no beer to be brought into the works, except a small amount which was brought in by the workers' relatives with the meals. Mr. Livesey attended at the works every Monday morning to give any of the workers who thought they had been wrongfully dismissed an opportunity of putting before him their side of the case. So far as I remember there were very few cases in which the foremen's decision was overruled.

Another of Mr. Livesey's ideas was a system of payment by results. This worked as follows : There were two twelve-hour shifts, one by day and one by night (we had no eight-hour day then), and if the men on both of the shifts made a specified number of cubic feet of gas during the week, each man working in the retort house would receive an extra 2s. 6d. on Monday night.

I only missed getting this extra money on two occasions. We were allowed soft soap with which to wash our hands, until it was discovered that some of the men took it out of the works and sold it.

Every Christmas the men were made a present of several pounds of meat each, but this privilege was lost through the same abuse of it as of the soft soap. A week's holiday was allowed to men who had been employed by the concern for a year ; after two years' service a week's holiday and two weeks' pay were given, but it was made a condition that the men went somewhere into the country or the seaside for their holiday. This was a recognition of the hard nature of the work, and its effect on the health of the workers.

After I had been working for a while at this place I brought my wife and our twelve-months-old baby down to London. The infant was one of twins, a girl. The other, a boy, died at the age of six months. The house in which I was lodging had twelve rooms, and I was able to rent a furnished top room for five shillings a week for my family. The room was about eight feet by nine feet, and I remember that there was not much room, either at the side of the bed or at its foot. There was just sufficient for a table and the cooking utensils. Three months after moving into this garret of a room my second daughter was born.

At this time I never dreamt that within ten years I would be in conflict with the great Mr. George Livesey and his company, as a result of a vicious system which he tried to introduce in 1889. I will deal with this later when I come to this strike, one of the biggest and most interesting of the period, that took place immediately after the formation of the union in 1889.

I was one of the junior workers, and when summer came and some of the retorts were shut down, I was dismissed.

I sold up what little home we had, and took the wife and the two children back to Birmingham to live with her parents at Swan Village.

I soon got work again at the Saltley works, handling a charging machine, the same one I had left the year before as a result of the strike. Swan Village was about seven miles from the works, and as there were no early workmen's trams or trains in those days, it meant being up at four o'clock in the morning to be at work by six.

After a few months—five, I think—the winter season began, and more retorts were put into commission.

The same Welsh foreman who had precipitated the strike the year before wanted to impose more work on us again. It was impossible to do the task demanded of us, and after a few days' discussion, with a view to getting the amount of work we were asked to do reduced, we declared a strike. Again we were not supported by all our workmates, for if they had stood by us, we would have had our grievance seen to.

I was infuriated by the conduct of these men, and told them they were a lot of " dumb dogs " and a few other choice things.

After leaving the Saltley works, my thoughts turned again to London. I found two companions, brothers by the name of Keegan, and started out again to walk the long road to the city. As on my first trip, I had little money, and my Irish friends were as poor as I was.

Arriving in London, we walked about for three days, and then I remembered an old friend of mine who had been in one of the strikes with me at the Saltley works. He was now a stage foreman at the Beckton Gas Works. We paid a visit to the works, found this old friend, Frank Kilroy, and he fixed us all up with jobs in the coke cellar.

At this works the coke was drawn out of the retorts below the coal cellar, and to cool the coke water was thrown on it and then the steaming coke was thrown out on to big heaps, taken in trucks to the pier-head, dumped into barges that were then taken to different parts of the country.

I had been used to scoop work, and after a few days I was put on " driving," for which I received extra pay. The awkward construction of the retort house made the work harder and hotter than any of the other gas works that I had worked in.

Most of the workers at Beckton lived at Canning Town, where I obtained lodgings, in Lawrence Street, with some Irish people. We were charged 4d. per day for being brought to and from the works by train, a distance of about four miles. This was a big improvement on the long walks to and from work that I had hitherto been used to.

After a while I took two furnished rooms in the same street and brought my wife and three children down from Birmingham to live with me again.

I was only receiving 5s. 4d. a day at the time, so I resolved to become a teetotaler until I was in a position to get enough money together to furnish a home. This is the pledge I signed :—

" TEMPERANCE PLEDGE

I Promise by Divine Assistance to abstain from all intoxicating Liquors and Beverages.

(Signed) WILLIAM THORNE.
THOMAS TUGG (Visitor).

September 8th, 1885."

I kept this pledge for over seven years, and even after I broke it I became, and have remained, a moderate drinker.

In those days I was a member of the Social Democratic Federation. At that time there were only about fourteen members, and we held our meetings at the house of one of the members, in Lansdowne Road, Canning Town. A good deal of propaganda work was done in different parts of the borough of West Ham.

Our favourite meeting-place was at the Beckton Road corner, a spot that has become historically famous through strike meetings and political demonstrations. Meetings are still held there two or three times a week.

The working class knew little of Socialism at that time. They were led by the other political parties— and their own ignorance—into being hostile to us, and we met with a great deal of opposition.

Often our opponents attempted violence, and we were told that we were talking a lot of nonsense, and that the idea of Socialism and its principles could never be accepted in this country.

Despite this hostility we stuck to our work ; we kept up our meetings and distributed literature, both at the meetings and at the houses in West Ham.

The fruit of our work was shown thirty-five years later, when Ramsay MacDonald, who subscribed to our principles, became the Prime Minister of Great Britain.

For the next few years I attended many political meetings in different parts of London, and in this way I came into personal contact with Charles Bradlaugh and Annie Besant, who were at that time lecturing for the Free Thought Movement.

Many times I have attended the Hall of Science in Old Street, when Bradlaugh was debating with some of the Freethinkers' strongest opponents ; he was a very clever and able debater, and few people ever scored a point off him in the debates.

Our cause was growing. I was appointed secretary of the Canning Town branch of the Social Democratic Federation. I only held this position for a short time, but during my time in this position I had my first meeting with Tom Mann. He came down to speak for us at Beckton Road corner.

It was a Sunday morning. I had been asked to take the chair for Tom. It was the first time I had ever spoken on a public platform, but being an enthusiast I felt that I could talk for at least a half-hour. To my great surprise, when I had been on the rostrum only a few short minutes I was at a loss to find anything to say, and so I at once called upon Tom Mann to address the meeting on the principles of Social Democracy. Tom was a wonderful speaker ; one of the most powerful and convincing men I have ever heard on a platform.

George Bernard Shaw made his first appearance amongst us in the East End at about this time. He was a member of the Fabian Society, and came down to lecture for the local branch of the S.D.F. Although the meeting had been well advertised, not more than thirty members of the general public turned up at the meeting.

I was the chairman at this meeting, and after it was

over I had a long talk to Shaw. He asked me about the progress of our cause in Canning Town, and we had a very interesting conversation about the current development of Socialism. He told me that he thought it would take a long time to make our cause popular in the country.

His lecture, while very interesting, was couched in such language as to make it difficult for his meaning to be grasped by most of the audience. He spoke to us just as if he was talking to an audience of thousands of people in the Albert Hall. I remember his sharp, caustic criticisms, and the keen flashes of wit, which, however, were mostly lost on his hearers.

The East End of London has never taken kindly to the " highbrows," although the growth of education is gradually permitting the submerged workers of this crowded, over-worked and over-populated district to appreciate the finer things of life.

We were now beginning to widen the scope of our propaganda efforts—the Executive Council of the Social Democratic Federation decided to run a number of meetings each Sunday morning, and the corner of Dod Street, Limehouse, was one of the spots chosen. The I.L.P. was not yet in existence, and we were the only people who were doing any real Socialist propaganda work. The police and many other people were becoming alarmed at our activity. We were making ourselves felt, and our numbers were growing rapidly.

Amongst our speakers and workers were the late H. M. Hyndman, Jack Williams, Eleanore Marx-Aveling, Dr. Aveling, John Burns—the first working man to become a Cabinet Minister in Great Britain—Harry Quelch, Herbert Burrows, William Morris, and Jack Ward, now Colonel J. Ward, who was Member of Parliament for Stoke.

After the first of these series of meetings the police intervened and attempted to prevent any more meetings being held. But this intervention did not deter us ; huge crowds of people turned up, and at each meeting the police would arrest the speakers. At first they were arrested and bound over, but finally, in August, 1885, Jack Williams was sentenced to a month's imprisonment. At the end of September of the same year the police gave in—Scotland Yard withdrew their restrictions on our meetings. They felt that we were getting too much advertisement, not alone in London, but all over the country.

To celebrate this victory for free speech, we organised a great demonstration at the West India Dock Gates. It was held on Sunday, September 27th, 1885. Over 50,000 people were present. Dr. Aveling was one of the chief speakers. He was one of our advanced men, a forceful intellectual. I was the chairman of one of the several platforms.

We had further meetings of this character, one at the "World's End," Chelsea, another at Enfield, where we held our meetings on Saturday nights. It was not the police that interfered with us here, but the people who broke up our meeting. I was asked to go there one evening; I went and had a rough time. As soon as the meeting started I was knocked off the chair that was used as a platform, and generally man-handled. We stuck to these meetings and in the end were allowed to carry on without molestation.

Early in the new year great numbers of workers and their families were suffering the torture of unemployment. A big meeting was arranged to be held in Trafalgar Square on February 8th, 1886.

Exciting scenes took place at this meeting, accompanied by rioting, but this was not the end of the unemployment agitation. John Burns, H. H. Champion, H. M. Hyndman, and Jack Williams were summoned for "seditious conspiracy" in connection with these riots. They were tried at the Old Bailey, and acquitted, on April 10th, 1886.

A year later, on November 13th, 1887, another meeting was held at Trafalgar Square in connection with a phase of the Irish question. Scotland Yard prohibited the meeting, but that did not deter us.

The Canning Town Branch of the S.D.F. hired a two-horse brake to drive to the meeting. We proceeded from Canning Town towards Trafalgar Square, and when we arrived at Ludgate Circus, the crowds converging on the Square were beginning to cause congestion, so we decided to get out and walk, leaving the brake on the Embankment to wait for us.

Other contingents from different parts of London were swinging along, and our little crowd was in the front. When we arrived at Wellington Street, Strand, policemen were stretched four deep across the road. We were within a few yards of this cordon, when the policemen, at a command, drew their truncheons and made a charge at us. It was a ferocious onslaught. Many of our people were badly injured, and I got a nasty tap on the head. Being defenceless, we scattered in all directions, finally working our way round to Trafalgar Square. When we arrived at the Square it was packed with policemen.

The Mayor of Westminster was there, waiting to read the Riot Act should the trouble become more serious. The Ambulance Corps was standing by.

We did not suffer as much as the contingent that came from the south side. They got a severe beating and many more casualties. I believe that one of their number was killed.

We returned to our brake on the Embankment, angry at what had happened.

Several of the workers at the gas works were Irishmen, and I heard much talk of Home Rule for Ireland. I attended a meeting at the St. James' Hall, and heard the great Stewart Parnell describe the deplorable conditions of the people in Ireland. He was a fiery and effective speaker and gained many supporters to his demand for Home Rule. He was supported by such able men as Joe Biggar, J. Sexton and William Harcourt.

Always on the side of the persecuted and downtrodden, I became an advocate, in my own rough way, for this cause. I addressed several meetings at Beckton Road corner on the subject. It was a hazardous job, because the workers knew little or nothing of the question. The newspapers opposed it, a suspicion of Irishmen had been created, and it was highly dangerous to speak too much about Home Rule.

At that time I little thought that I should become a Member of Parliament for the Plaistow Division of West Ham, and be in the House of Commons when the Home Rule Bill was passed and a free Constitution granted to Ireland.

I remember a friend, Pat Murphy—a stoker from the Silvertown Gas Works—carrying on an animated discussion with me and attacking me for my views on Labour questions. We were talking about Socialism and Home Rule. Pat was a Nationalist, a Home Ruler and a Catholic. I was winning the argument and Pat got wild.

" Shut up, you are a materialist ! " he roared at me, at the same time giving me a terrible slap on the jaw.

In a second there were two of us in the fight, and we banged each other about for some time. I knocked his head against a window pane and broke the glass, and he gave me a blow that knocked me against the mantelshelf and cut my eye. Then I dropped on to the fender and cut my knee. I gave in to his energetic method of advocacy, but neither of us could go to work for a day or two.

We did not spoil our friendship by this little disagreement.

Great suffering was being felt as a result of the large number of unemployed at this time. Women and children were starving, especially in Old Canning Town, Tidal Basin and Custom House areas of Dockland. There were no local authorities that could feed these necessitous people. The work of men like George Lansbury and Will Crooks for the starving poor of the East End of London had not yet started. So I, with

a few comrades, decided to make an effort to feed the
children at least.

On Saturday nights we would visit butchers, bakers
and greengrocers, and ask them to give us bread and
materials for making soup. They were all very generous, and we took the food to a temperance bar at 144,
Barking Road, where the man, named Zibach, who ran
the place, allowed us to use a copper he had to make
soup in. A notice was put up stating that the children
would be fed at 9.30 on Sunday morning.

A more pitiable, heartbreaking sight than those poor
ill-clothed children, coming along in the cold and biting
winds, cannot be imagined. Sweet, tender young
things, they were like ravenous wolves. So hungry
were they, it was difficult to keep them in order while
they were being served. We gave them all a good
basin of soup, but they all wanted to be fed at once.

It was very unpleasant work in some ways, but we
had the satisfaction of knowing that we had done our
best to provide these little kiddies with food for part of
the week, and ease for a short while the gnawing pain
in their little stomachs.

This sort of thing was breeding rebels and opponents
to a system that permitted the poor to starve in the
East End while in the West End others satisfied their
appetites with luxurious meals amidst the greatest
comfort.

CHAPTER IV

THE BIRTH OF MY UNION

Out of evil comes good. The despair of the workers at the conditions they were compelled to put up with was causing a stirring in their souls—souls deadened by long hours of hard labour, rewarded with the smallest possible amount of money to provide sufficient food, clothing and shelter to enable them to continue their drudging toil. Employers with no thought for the lives of their workers were unconsciously creating the cause of their own destruction. An unrest was growing that only wanted leadership and opportunity to become a potent force.

Attempts were made to form a union of gas workers and general labourers. The first attempt was in 1884. Jack Monk was the hero of this effort, but so strong was the economic control of the employers over the lives of the workers that the " Association," as it was called, lasted but a few short weeks. During that time the fear of victimisation was so great that all connected with it had to act secretly. Jack veiled his identity behind the name of " Julien."

In the following year another attempt was made. A society was formed and my old friend George Angle was appointed secretary. Its headquarters were at the " Sir John Lawerence," Canning Town. The fear of the boss, and other causes, were against the success of this venture and the society died after a few months.

I was not disheartened. I was only a common labourer, with a very limited education, but I had hope, and God gave me courage. I kept agitating ; I kept preaching the gospel of unity, and proclaiming that simple justice was our right.

During my spare time between drawing and charging the retorts at the Beckton Gas Works, I used to talk to the men—in the lobby, in the mess-room, or wherever opportunity permitted. I knew that without a trade union the workers could do little, that we would be compelled to submit to any kind of tyranny, or any conditions that the engineer chose to force upon us through the foreman. I was anxious to get a union formed, so that our grievances—and they were many—could be rectified.

My zeal attracted attention. The foreman often told me that I was risking dismissal by continuing to carry on my agitation in the works and on the street corners. I did not care. I had a goal, an aim, a message. I told the foreman, and other well-meaning friends, that I had the right to talk to men as I thought proper in my spare time, and that whether I got the " sack " or not I would not give up my active work.

Nevertheless, I was careful ; I gave the foreman no chance to " sack " me. I was a good timekeeper and I gave, so far as my work was concerned, no cause for complaint.

I had a wife and children to think of as well, and I knew the employers' greatest ally was the fear of starvation. I kept on with my agitation ; I gathered friends who believed in me and helped me ; I got into small troubles, even with the police, but I persevered ; my courage grew.

One day the resident engineer came into the retort house where I was working, and asked me : " What is this Socialism I hear you are always talking about to the men ? "

I had in my pocket a copy of John Burns' speech which he delivered from the dock at the Old Bailey, on January 18th, 1888, when he was charged with seditious conspiracy. I stood with my foot on a pile of coal, with the flashing light of the retorts athwart

the paper, and above the noise of the works I declaimed
John Burns' words :—

" Socialism is a theory of society which advocates
a more just, orderly, and harmonious arrangement of
the social relations of mankind than that which
prevails now.

" Substituting the principle of association for that
of competition in every branch of production and
distribution, Socialism proposes to abolish the system
of wage slavery, and establish instead governmental,
municipal co-operation, securing to every honest
worker the full value of his labour, partly in personal
remuneration, and partly in social and public benefits,
such as education and recreation, sustenance and
care in old age.

" Socialism proposes that labour shall be a noble
elevating duty, not an unhealthy slavish drudgery."

He listened to me and asked me where I had
" learned all this foolish rubbish." I told him that I
had learnt from books and pamphlets that I bought
with the few shillings I had to spare ; that I had learnt
it in the works where I had been employed ; that I had
learnt it from bitter experience. He left me without
replying or asking further questions.

One of the books that had helped me to form my
criticism of society and to shape my ideas was called
" A Review of European Society, and an Exposition
and Vindication of the Principles of Social Democracy,"
written by Mr. J. Sketchley. This book gave statistics
of the fighting forces in the different countries, and the
large amount of money spent on maintaining them, and
at the same time it contrasted the deplorable conditions
under which the wage earners lived. Something could
be done by Parliament I thought, but not as it was
then constituted, with every interest except labour
adequately represented. I was convinced that radical
changes would have to be made, and the franchise for

both men and women broadened, and to these ends I devoted some of my propaganda efforts.

The need for these changes and reforms was, however, not as pressing as those demanding attention in the workshop, for here the employers were rapidly creating the conditions that were giving the workers only the alternative of servile submission to tyranny of the worst kind and abject wage slavery, or of uniting in some form of combination and compelling just and fair consideration of their views on the wages and conditions under which they should work.

Anything to save money or labour was seized upon by our employers, irrespective of its effects on the workers. The Gas Company decided to introduce the " iron man " into their works. This was the compressed-air machine, for drawing and charging the retorts, which caused me to leave the Birmingham Gas Works, sell my home, and walk to London. The company had been getting glowing reports from different parts of the country where these wage-saving machines had been introduced and, naturally, they were anxious to follow suit. Machinery had made rapid developments during this period in all factories and works, and in all cases it was being introduced only because it reduced the wages bill, and in spite of the fact that it put more and more unemployed workers on the labour market.

I was one of the first men asked to work on one of these machines, perhaps because the foreman had heard that I had worked one in Birmingham. The same number of men was selected to work the machines as at Birmingham. The number of retorts that had to be charged and drawn for a day's work was fixed by the foreman, without in any way consulting the men who had to work them.

I talked to my companions about my previous experience and told them that the task allotted to us was more than we could do. With one of my companions, I was appointed to make representations to the stage foreman, but our view got no hearing and had no effect. After this I told the men that, as we had no union behind us for the purpose of negotiating a reasonable day's work for the payment received, the best thing would be to take the best terms and conditions possible.

We started to work with the machines, but they did not work properly. Breakdown after breakdown occurred, which made us busier even than if the machines had been perfect. It meant that many nights we did not get a chance to eat our food. We found that the machines made our work much harder and gave us less time for a rest than the hand work. In fact, we became like parts of a machine ourselves. But trouble was coming, for there is a limit to all things.

A system was introduced in each retort house, a system which I termed " inhuman competition for the benefit of the directors and shareholders of the company, and to the disadvantage of the men." This system was worked through the foremen. There were two general foremen, one for the twelve-hour day shift, and one for the twelve-hour night shift ; under these men were the stage foremen in each retort house.

The foreman would visit the meter house and check the number of cubic feet of gas that was being made each hour by the opposite shifts. If it was found that one shift was not making as much gas as the other, the head foremen would go at once to the stage foremen, who would see that the stokers speeded up and got more coal into the retorts and more coke out. These incidents made me understand the full significance of the term " wage slave."

Another way of speeding up was adopted. Ten charges was either a day or a night's work—five charges, a long rest, and then another five charges. The foremen, at the behest of their superiors, would drive to push the charges along so as to get the first five in as early as ten o'clock, and, being an hour ahead of time, would want an extra charge put in. This system was continued until a big event took place that I will relate shortly.

In the meantime, I was agitating to get the men a week's holiday. I had a petition drafted by an old friend of mine, with a view to getting the men to sign it, and then I proposed to place it before the resident engineer.

Most of the men working on my shift signed it, but, to my surprise and disgust, the men on the other shift would not. I believe the foreman had persuaded them not to.

I felt deeply about this, for my object was to create an appetite for more and more concessions, and then to form a trade union and fight for the eight-hour day.

The time of the formation of a union was approaching rapidly. It was precipitated by the introduction of a practice by which the stage foremen would come to certain men on Sunday morning and order them to stay on to do three extra charges. This meant that, instead of finishing at 5.30, the men had to work right through until ten or eleven o'clock.

Generally the men had no food, because when they left home they did not know that they would have to stay on and work later. There was a big canteen adjacent to the works, where sometimes food and drink were obtainable, but when the eighteen-hour shift was finished, the men living at Poplar and Canning Town, as most of them did, had a walk of nearly four miles. This caused a great deal of annoyance and, on top of the other slave-driving methods, caused the men to get desperate. They were almost prepared to go on strike, even though they had no union behind them. I saw the time was ripe; the day that I had waited for so long had at last dawned. This was the psychological moment for forming the union.

A few of us got together; I gave them my views, and we held a meeting. This was on March 31st, 1889. The meeting was held at the present site of the Canning Town Public Hall.

A resolution was passed in favour of a gas workers' union being formed, with the eight-hour day as one of its objects. With George Angle and George Gilby, I was elected as a delegate to represent my shift. The opposite shift was represented by four other men, Hutchings, Mack, Gundy, and Mansfield — God bless their brave hearts !

Prior to the meeting we interviewed all the men in the different parts of the works, and asked them if they were in favour of a union being established at Beckton without pledging themselves to join it. The answers were very favourable.

Sunday morning, March 31st, 1889—a lovely sunny morning—was the birthday of the National Union of Gas Workers and General Labourers of Great Britain and Ireland. To-day it is the largest union of its kind in the world.

A big enthusiastic crowd turned up. I led a contingent from Barking to the meeting place, with a band that I paid for out of my own pocket. We had an old van for a platform. Dear old Ben Tillett was with us, with his new-found powers of oratory ; Harry Hobart, Dick Mansfield, George Angle, and one or two other good fighters were the speakers, with myself.

The atmosphere was electric when I mounted the platform. "Fellow wage slaves, I am more than pleased to see such a big crowd of workers and friends from the Beckton Gas Works," was my greeting to them. The reply was a heartening cheer, and my stage fright disappeared. Then I talked to them like this :

"I know that many of you have been working eighteen hours under very hard and difficult circumstances, that many of you must be dead tired ; often have I done the eighteen-hour shift. I am under the impression that the resident engineer knew that I had arranged this meeting, and that he deliberately kept you working late. This sort of thing has gone on for a long time ; we have protested, but time after time we have been sneered at, ignored and have secured no redress. Let me tell you that you will never get any alteration in Sunday work, no alteration in any of your conditions or wages, unless you join together and form a strong trade union. Then you will be able to have a voice and say how long you will work, and how much you will do for a day's work.

" In my opinion, you have a perfect right to discuss all these matters with your employer through your chosen spokesman. Why should any employer have the power to say you must do this, that, and the other thing. By your labour power you create useful things for the community, you create wealth and dividends, but you have no say, no voice, in any of these matters.

" All this can be altered if you will join together and form a powerful union, not only for gas workers, but one that will embrace all kinds of general labourers. Some of you only work in the gas works in the winter ; when the warm weather comes, you are dismissed, to find what work you can get at the docks, in the brickfields, navvying, or anything that comes along.

" Stand together this time ; forget the past efforts we have made to form you into a union, when we failed only because you did not respond to our call. Some of you were afraid of your own shadows, but this morning I want you to swear and declare that you mean business and that nothing will deter you from your aim.

" It is easy to break one stick, but when fifty sticks are together in one bundle it is a much more difficult job. The way you have been treated at your work for many years is scandalous, brutal, and inhuman. I pledge my word that, if you will stand firm and don't waver, within six months we will claim and win the eight-hour day, a six-day week, and the abolition of the present slave-driving methods in vogue not only at the Beckton Gas Works, but all over the country. Now, will you do this ? "

There was one loud roar of " We will ! " That yell was the last birth pain of the union. I knew that the men meant business. I told them that I was satisfied, that I was only a rough diamond, that I could not talk as fluently as some of my colleagues, but I knew what we wanted and was prepared to fight for it. I warned the men not to give the foremen any chance to complain at them for losing time, and I made an energetic appeal to them to attend to their work in the usual way and give no opportunity for any of them to be victimised.

Dear comrade and great fighter, Ben Tillett spoke to the men after I had finished. His was an eloquent speech, militant and persuasive. I believe he had a slight impediment of speech at the time. He told of his own efforts to organise the dock workers, and the little response the men made. He had, however, formed an organisation known as the Tea Operatives' and Dock Workers' Union, that I remained a member of until my own organisation came into being. Tillett described the horrible conditions under which the dockers worked, and was disappointed at the small response they made ; but their time was to come in the very near future. He told the men how glad he was to help " Mr. Thorne " to form a sound and genuine union, and the friendship that existed between us.

Harry Hobart, a member of the S.D.F. and a compositor, addressed the meeting, and gave the men the result of his experience as a member of the London Society of Compositors. It was useful advice, and well heeded. Another man, just a common gas worker like myself, but a good speaker and a well-read man, Jack Walsh, also urged the men to get into the union.

After the speeches were over, I called for volunteers to form an organising committee, of which George Angle was appointed the secretary ; then we started to take down the names of the men who wanted to join up. Eight hundred joined that morning. The entrance fee was 1s., and we had to borrow several pails to hold the coppers and other coins that were paid in. Beside Clem Edwards, Ben Tillett, W. Byford—who later became my father-in-law through my second marriage— George Angle, the first branch secretary, Mark Hutchings, Dick Mansfield, the chief delegate, all helped to take down the names.

The meeting over, we had to get down to business. Ben Tillett, Byford, and myself formed ourselves into a " provisional committee " to draft a set of rules and to discuss ways and means of getting enrolled in the union the workers in the other gas works around London. Byford was made treasurer. He was the proprietor of a temperance bar at 144, Barking Road. He had a good knowledge of trade union administration, because for many years he had been secretary of the Yorkshire Glass Bottle Workers' Association.

I was highly elated at our success. The news of the meeting spread like wildfire ; in the public-houses, factories, and works in Canning Town, Barking, East and West Ham every one was talking about the union. Soon my first doubts as to whether the union would succeed were dispelled ; the men were solid, enthusiastic, and anxious to get all their mates enrolled.

I had to return to my work that Sunday night, as I had been on the day shift the previous week. The men at the works could talk about nothing else but " the union " and what it was going to do.

We had not got the contribution cards printed yet, but the men were as keen as mustard. I directed all my talk to the question of establishing the eight-hour day. The provisional committee sat from time to time, directing propaganda and attending to routine and administration work. Instructions were given to hold meetings in different parts of London to organise those that were not yet in the union.

Sunday after Sunday we would start out from 144,

Barking Road, our headquarters, to encourage the men at other gas works. As many as twenty brake loads of workers would go out on these Sunday morning crusades. The idea caught on ; enthusiasm was at a high pitch, and within two weeks we had over 3,000 men in the union.

Never before had men responded like they did. For months London was ablaze. The newspapers throughout the country were giving good reports of our activities. They were curious to know what we wanted and what we were going to do.

I knew what we were going to do. I kept in mind all the time my pledge to the men at the first meeting. To work and fight for the eight-hour day—that was my first objective, soon to be won.

We had plenty of assistance. Ben Tillett, Tom Mann, Jack Burns, Harry Hobart, Harry Quelch, and Herbert Burrowes were our stalwarts ; their voices were heard at many meetings and from many platforms.

The provisional committee decided to call the union the " National Union of Gas Workers and General Labourers." We had a big debate on the amount of contributions to be paid. I pleaded for 2d. per week ; others pleaded for more, but 2d. was the sum finally agreed upon. We took as our motto " Love, Unity, and Fidelity " ; our slogan was " One Man, One Ticket, and every Man with a Ticket." The ticket was the union card.

Hampered by our ignorance of trade union methods, we pushed on. The contribution cards were ready, money was coming in fast, the membership was increasing by leaps and bounds. The provisional committee had drafted a code of rules, that was to be endorsed by a delegate meeting. At this meeting we found that the general secretary's salary had been fixed at £2 10s. per week. This the delegates altered to £2 5s.

The fighting spirit was strong in the delegates ; it was proposed to petition the directors of the different companies in London for an advance of 1s. per day in the wages of all their workers. I opposed this; I wanted a reduction in the working hours. "Shorten the hours and prolong your lives," was my plea. I declared that the eight-hour day would not alone mean a reduction of four hours a day for the workers then employed, but that it meant a large number of unemployed would be absorbed, and so reduce the inhuman competition that was making men more like beasts than civilised persons. I won the day.

A petition was drafted and signed and sent to the companies demanding the Eight-Hour Working Day. We agreed that the men at no one gas works, under the control of any one company, should accept the eight-hour day until it had been agreed that a uniform amount of work should be done in the eight hours by all works. We were quite aware that we would have to do more work per hour under the eight-hour day than we did under the twelve-hour day.

Weeks passed by and no reply came from the companies to our demand. The men were getting impatient. A spirit of revolt was growing. Then I received word that the directors of the Gas Light and Coke Company had conceded the eight-hour day, and only the question of making arrangements about the number of retorts to be drawn and charged in each eight hours was left to be dealt with.

We had several discussions with the resident engineer, and finally came to a settlement for the Beckton Gas Works; the men employed at the other works of the Company were satisfied with the terms we had secured, except at the Nine Elms Works. At this works the engineer wanted the men to do more work than we had arranged for, and actually more than was humanly possible; we refused to start work until Nine Elms got a settlement. The men there sent for me, and after a discussion lasting over two hours with the engineer we got what we wanted.

I wish my readers could have seen the joy in the smiling faces of the men and the delegates when I reported our victory—that we had won the eight-hour day. It was a milestone in trade union history, and one of the greatest victories ever achieved. It gave the lead to many other workers in Great Britain and other countries.

The formation of our union, and its first victory, put heart into thousands of unskilled, badly paid and unorganised workers. It led to big developments that I was concerned in that I shall tell of later.

A delegate meeting was summoned to be held on May 20th, when it was decided that nominations should be received for the position of general secretary of the union, and a vote taken which was returnable not later than June 24th. I was asked to stand for the position. I hesitated for some time, knowing my educational limitations, but I knew that what I lacked in education I could make up by my knowledge of the industrial movements.

Ben Tillett was also asked by some of the men to run for the position, not because of any ill-feeling against me, but because of his knowledge of clerical and book-keeping work and the good service he had given so freely in helping to get the union started. Tillett was not anxious to run ; he saw that the time was rapidly approaching when the dockers, whom he had been trying to organise for some time, would be ready to answer the call. Our success had lit the torch of trade unionism that was in the next few months to flame in every part of the country. Tillett's foresight was soon to be vindicated.

We had a friendly chat about the matter, and we both agreed to go to the ballot. The voting took two weeks to complete and on June 26th, 1889, the result was made known by the scrutineers. It was :—

THORNE	.	.	.	. 2,296
TILLETT	.	.	.	. 69
Majority	.	.	. 2,227

I was authorised to begin my new and important duties as general secretary of the union on July 1st.

A week's notice was the custom at the gas works, so I visited the resident engineer on Friday before beginning my duties on the Monday, and asked him if the week's notice could be foregone as I wanted to get to my new job.

He said : " Oh, yes, but you will soon be out of your new berth. Your union will be like many others that have sprung up like a mushroom over night, and then the members have dropped away like leaves in autumn."

I told him that he was mistaken this time. " Do you know," I said, " that you are to some extent responsible for the formation of the union ? " He was curious. " I don't see how," he said. " Well, if you are not directly responsible," I told him, " you indirectly helped us by the slave-driving methods you have brought into the retort houses for some time past. Your system of getting the foremen to drive the stage foremen, who, in turn, drive the stokers, has had the effect of stirring the men."

" Well," he said, " I have to visit the meter house from time to time to see if one shift of men has made more gas than the other, and if they have I am bound to complain to the shift foreman whose men have not made as much gas."

" Exactly, and that is the cause of the agitation that has been going on," I told him.

He let me go and told me that at any time I wanted to come back he would give me a job in the works, because he had heard that, although I was a consistent and persistent agitator, I had always done my work well and had been a good timekeeper.

I thanked him for letting me get away and said a last good-bye to manual labour in the gas works.

The following month, on July 17th, 1889, a concert was organised by the men working on the No. 3 shift to celebrate the securing of the eight-hour day, and to present me with a silver watch and chain and an address. It was particularly pleasing that this happy little function was promoted by the No. 3 shift, because under the twelve-hour day there had only been two shifts.

The address was worded in these terms :—

" This Address, together with a watch and chain, has been presented to William Thorne, General Secretary of the National Union of Gas Workers and General Labourers of Great Britain and Ireland, by the Workmen of No. 3 Shift, Carbonising Department, Beckton Gas Works, as a humble token in recognition of the invaluable services he has rendered to the Gas Workers of the United Kingdom, and to the Cause of Labour Generally.

" A Champion of the Rights of Labour, from his boyhood, his Untiring Energy, his Manly Courage, his earnest Advocacy, and his Honesty of Purpose in the Cause of Trade Unionism, has gained for him Admiration and Respect of all ranks in the Army of Labour.

" On behalf of the Committee,
" J. MACK, *Treasurer*.
" OWEN CRUMMY, *Secretary*."

My second eldest daughter recited at the concert, and I was asked to make a speech, in which I thanked them for the honour they had conferred on me in electing me general secretary of the union. " Nothing will be wanting on my part," I told them, " to make the union a great success, and by the assistance and co-operation of the members failure is unthinkable."

I reminded the men of the great victory we had secured in the eight-hour day, the abolition of the twelve-hour day without any reduction in wages.

Our success in London had been broadcasted throughout the country. Workers everywhere were asking about the union and how they could join it. I told the men this, and explained what a heavy task it meant for me, with my lack of education. I was, however, given assistance by my friends, and particularly by the acting treasurer, Mr. W. Byford.

I thanked the donors for the present they gave. I have received many others since, but there is none I prize more, and there is no incident in my life that I look back on with greater pleasure than that simple but happy function. It was more historic than we thought of or even realise now.

The formation of our union was the definite establishment, and the beginning, of what has been termed the " New Unionism." It was the culmination of long years of Socialist propaganda amongst the underpaid and oppressed workers. Politics had been preached to them, vague indefinite appeals to revolution, but we offered them something tangible, a definite, clearly-lighted road out of their misery, a trade ·union that would improve their wages and conditions ; that would protect them from petty tyranny of employers. They saw for the first time the light, and groping out of the darkness of the degradation that the growing industrialism had thrown them into, they grasped firmly and started to climb the ladder of their emancipation. They came in thousands, within six months we had made over 20,000 members in different parts of the country. We showed the way to the dockers and other unskilled workers; our example and our success gave them hope. Within a short time the " New Unionism " was in full flower. It changed the whole face of the British Trade Union Movement, a movement that had mainly consisted of reformist, liberal-minded craftsmen and skilled unionists. The growth and development of our union and the dockers and others that followed us brought to the Trade Union Congress a new force, clear-sighted and virile. It rejuvenated the industrial trade union movement. It established on a firm footing the political Labour Movement ; gave it an impetus that has carried it to its present strength and power in the land, and brought about the harmonious co-operation between the two that has never been severed. It was this spirit of the " New Unionism " that made international working-class solidarity a reality, and, strange to say, the historians hardly notice the revolution we created. Our advent was not as spectacular as the great dock strike that I am coming to shortly ; the immensity of that epic struggle and the magnetic characters that flashed through it overshadowed, and even blinded, men like Sidney Webb, when he drew his conclusions in his monumental work on the History of Trade Unionism. Still, we did not fight for history, praise, or to secure kudos. It was the lives of our people and their bread and butter we were thinking of. We were struggling to lift ourselves out of the slime of poverty into the fresh air of freedom. That we achieved in a measure, and greater achievements are ahead.

CHAPTER V

THE BIG DOCK STRIKE

MY new duties as secretary of the union brought longer hours, and an even greater strain on my mental and physical resources, than the hard labour of the gas works. But I was working for more than wages. I was working for the lives of men, women and children. The work was as a religion, a holy mission. I gloried in it.

I had only been in my new post a few weeks when, just before lunch on a Saturday, the great John Burns walked into my office at 144, Barking Road.

" Hello, Jack ! What brings you down this way ? "
I knew that he lived at Battersea.

" Oh," he said, " I am down and out, and having a look around. I thought I would call in and see how you were getting along with your new work."

Burns congratulated me on my election to the secretaryship of the union, and asked me whether I could manage the work. I told him that I would work day and night, if it was necessary, to give satisfaction to the members. I told him how I was getting outside help with regard to the book-keeping, and that the treasurer, Mr. Byford, who had trade union secretarial experience, would guide me in other matters. I showed him some of the many letters that I had received during the week, asking for an organiser to come to different places to give information about the union. We had no organisers then, and many of the letters were asking for interpretations about the different rules. I was taxed to give the right definition to many of these queries.

Burns remarked, " You have a tough job on hand."

He saw the bad handwriting of most of the letters, and said, " Some of the writing is worse than yours, and that is bad enough." This was quite true, because I have never been a good writer, even to the present day. Burns also made some remark about the grammar and composition of the letters.

" What can you expect ? The writers of these letters are only rough and ready men," I told him. " Most of them gas workers that have had to start work very early in life, like their fathers before them. The sons of the craftsmen had a better chance, because their parents were much better off than the parents of these poor labourers."

" Well, I wish you the best of luck," said Burns, and made to say good-bye. It was just on dinner time, and I reminded him that he had told me that he was " down and out." I told him that my salary was only £2 5s. a week, and by then I had a wife and five children, and a rent of 8s. per week to pay. I was sorry that I could not do much for him, but he should come along with me and have some dinner.

When we arrived at my home my wife was surprised to see Burns. She had not met him before, but had heard a lot about him as a Socialist agitator, and his imprisonment in connection with the unemployed. My wife was a little upset, because she only had our usual Saturday meal of fish and chips—what we termed a " make-shift." However, it was the best we could offer, and we made Burns welcome. He enjoyed the meal, for I suppose he was quite hungry. After it was over we had a little talk, and he told me he was starting to walk back home to Battersea. I gave him 2s. to pay his fare with, we shook hands and he left.

At that time I hardly imagined that within seventeen years he would become a Member of Parliament and a Cabinet Minister ! I thought that he would most probably get put into jail for his agitation, for at the time he was full of fight.

Burns joined the Socialist movement about the middle of the 'eighties, he was a member of the executive of the Social Democratic Federation, and I came in contact with him quite a lot in the great dock strike. That I will deal with shortly.

The union was still making progress. By July, 1889, we had over sixty branches, forty-four in London, and over twenty provincial branches. We were getting inquiries from Ireland to start branches there, but this was not done until later. I was kept very busy visiting the branches and explaining and advising the men about the methods of conducting the branches and about the policy of the union. My trade union work dovetailed with my Socialist propaganda, and I never lost an opportunity to point the moral of any situation or circumstance.

We had gone outside the gas works with our organisation work, and had taken in many riverside and factory workers, quite a number in Silvertown, Jack Jones's Parliamentary constituency. In this work I met and came in contact with a large number of the dockers; many of them were members of the S.D.F. Their wages and conditions were appalling. A terrible unrest was rapidly growing amongst them, they wanted to be organised, they had seen what we had done with regard to securing the eight-hour day and many other smaller concessions; they wanted to join our union, but we had our hands full with the work of consolidating the gas workers and general labourers, and our aim had not been to organise dockers. I believe that nowhere in the world have white men had to endure such terrible conditions as those under which the dockers worked. The majority of them were only employed casually, taken on for an hour or two, or a day or two. Their wages were 5d. per hour. The stevedores, who were organised, had a better rate. The " call on," as the process of picking the men wanted was known, was a heartrending sight. Many able pens have attempted to describe the scene, but none more vivid or true than this short but graphic picture by Ben Tillett.*

". . . the last remnants of strength exerted in an effort to get work for an hour, a half-hour, for a few pence. Such strugglings, shoutings, cursings, with a grinning brute selecting the chosen of the poor wretches.

" At the ' cage ' so termed because of the stout iron bars made to protect the ' caller-on,' men ravening for food fought like madmen for the ticket, a veritable talisman of life. As a brute would throw scraps to hungry wolves to delight in the exhibition of the savage struggle for existence, with the beasts tearing each other to pieces, so these creatures would delight in the spectacle, which while it imbruted the victims of such a tragedy, impeached and cursed society. Coats, flesh, and even ears, were torn off, men were crushed to death in the struggle, helpless if fallen. The strong literally threw themselves over the heads of their fellows, and battled with kick and curse through the kicking, punching, cursing crowd to the rails of the cage, which held them like rats— mad, human rats, who saw food in the ticket. Calls at any period of the day or night kept men for a week at a time hungry and expectant for the food and the work which never came.

" Night and day watches, the scraping of refuse heaps, the furtive, miserly storing of refuse rice the coolies had thrown away, to keep body and soul together. Yet the full-blooded of the capitalists and the ' reformers ' could never see the cause of the effects of the capitalist system.

" Men would risk life for the boss who carried a ticket of employment ; no abasement was too abject, and so the petty tyrants flourished on a system promoting starvation and death.

* " A Brief History of the Dockers' Union, Commemorating the 1889 Dockers' Strike."

" There are memories of men who battled against hunger and exhaustion, dying as their greedy fingers clutched the few shillings which a day's labour had exacted, dropping dead at the pay-box. Others, and in multiplicity of martyrdom, dying after reaching home, every muscle and nerve-centre emptied of force. The driving and the foul language of foremen were a bitter curse to the men, and a blight on the most normal of decent feelings. There were pictures of dear women who died in pangs of childbirth on bare floors, cheerless, and without warmth when winter's malignant fingers clutched hungrily at the corpse.

" Strong men weep, and so the curse of living is accepted wolf-like, and so our fellow-creatures die without courage enough to wail a protest against the social murder."

This description is not exaggerated. I have seen such scenes many a time at Custom House, Connaught Road, at the main entrance to the Albert Docks, and other places in Dockland. The stevedores through their organisation had a better system, they were the aristocrats of the docks. Then there were what was known as the " Royals," a class of men that got preference over the mass. It was alleged that the " Royals " got their preference through a form of free-masonry, created by tipping the " caller-on."

Beside being general secretary, I was doing the work of the London district secretary. Our contributions were only 2d. per member, and finances had to be handled economically.

I worked day and night attending branch and public meetings. Even Sundays were not my own.

My wife often asked me whether I thought I would see the children before Sunday, when I always tried to have a little time at home, but I seldom did.

My early experience had developed the habit of early rising that I still practise, and when I came to my office at 7.30 each morning, the wife of the treasurer, Mrs. Byford—a fine old soul—would often say, " Why don't you stay here all night ? You don't seem to be away from the office many hours together." I might say that these were comparatively easy times, and when I see trade union secretaries to-day, who always get a full night's rest, and arrive at their offices between nine and ten o'clock in the morning, I wonder if it is fully realised what amount of labour and sacrifice was necessary to build up the Trade Union Movement to its present strength.

The union had put backbone into the men throughout the country. I was getting news almost every day about strikes in different places, strikes to rectify small and large grievances—many of them took place before the ink was dry on their contribution cards. Things were going well with us, but the dockers were chafing more and more under their conditions ; they appealed to me and to my colleagues to allow them to come into the union, but we could not take them. Ben Tillett had a union for them, the Tea Operatives' and Dock Workers' Union. Its membership rose and fell from a few hundreds, but no great move could be made. Tillett, Burns, Tom Mann, and others used to preach the gospel of manliness at the dock gates to them, but words had apparently little effect. It was our example and our achievement, both in forming our union and securing advantages through it, that opened their eyes, and then their great day came.

It was on Saturday, August 10th, 1889, that I received a telegram from one of my old pals, Will Harris, who worked on one of the tugs at the Albert Docks. He wanted me to meet him at the South Dock gates on the following Monday morning, and said that an effort was going to be made to organise the dockers and start a union for them.

I met him on the Sunday morning, and he told me he was particularly anxious to get me to come along, because of the success I had achieved in organising the gas workers in a union and securing the eight-hour day and other improvements for them. I arranged to meet him at 7.30 the next morning. When I arrived at the South Dock gates, who should I meet but my dear old friend Tom McCarthy, a stevedore. He was one of my best pals, and one of the greatest fighters in the Labour Movement at the time, although he has never received the full measure of recognition that he deserved.

The time of the " call-on " was eight o'clock. Tom got a chair from a coffee-shop close by. The chair was our platform, and was placed near where the men gathered and waited for the " call-on."

Tom mounted the chair and started the meeting ; he rubbed into the men the facts of the terrible conditions they worked under. He was in a position to do this, as he was a stevedore and had an intimate knowledge of the dockers' work. He was a fine platform speaker, and his Irish ancestry gave him a much-needed vein of humour.

I followed Tom with a speech in which I pointed out to the men what organisation had done for the gas workers. I backed up Tom's appeal to them to form a union and then refuse to go to work. Finally the proposition was put to a vote of the meeting, and every man voted to stay out. That was the beginning of the great dock strike of 1889, that for many months filled the news columns of every paper in the country, aye, of the civilised world—an eruption that shook the whole country.

The great dock strike, when it started, was not, as has often been stated, for the " dockers' tanner " and a more equitable " plus." It was a revolt at the general conditions. The demands on which the strike was settled, and which were later spoken of, were formulated actually during the strike. Our aim accomplished at South Dock gates, we marched these pioneer rebels to the Poplar Dock gates, and as we marched we gathered crowds of people. At Poplar another fine response was made to our appeal. We moved on to Custom House,

arriving about midday, just when the men were coming
out to their dinner. Little dinner they could get with
their miserable wages. There was a public-house just
opposite Custom House where the men would sit and
eat their scraps of bread and cheese, sometimes just
dry bread and a pot of four ale. At that time it was
a common practice among the workmen all over London
to call for a pot of four ale, and for three, four, or five
men to drink out of the same pot. Many of them,
most of them, in fact, could not afford a pot of their
own. This was talked of amongst us as " not paying
your corner." The men were, however, not looked upon
as spongers, but just " down and out."

The strike was started. The following day we continued our meetings. The numbers multiplied. By the
Wednesday Ben Tillett and Tom Mann were leading the
rebellion like supermen. The Stevedores' Union would
not join in at first. Tom McCarthy, who was on their
executive, fought for them to throw in their lot, but not
until the men themselves defied their leaders did official
support come. Tom McCarthy took their banner without permission, and it flew in front of many contingents
of men new-born to freedom in the struggle.

The strike was not three days old when over 10,000
men were out, and more and more joining every
minute. One by one the docks became deserted and
idle ; lightermen left their barges and craft ; tug
drivers, waterside workers, factory hands, carmen, coal
porters, sailors and firemen—all classes and categories
of workers were in the fight.

Tom Mann was like a streak of human quicksilver,
here, there, and everywhere, commanding, pleading,
cajoling, enthusing. Ben Tillett—the one man of the
period with a spark of genius and imagination—was
directing, leading. He had planned a picket system for
the whole fifty miles of London's docks.

John Burns had not yet entered the fight. He did
not come in until the strike was complete. After a few
days the strikers not picketing formed processions and

marched through the City. Gigantic meetings were held on Tower Hill. The whole north side of the river was in revolt. I was addressing meetings day and night, and watching my own affairs as well.

The new Labour Protection League, headed by Harry Quelch, composed of waterside and dock workers on the south side of the river, were with us. The strike was complete. The marine and contiguous traffic of the world's largest port was completely paralysed, and the world waited and wondered what was going to happen next.

A central strike committee was formed with the Stevedores' Union. It was held at " Wades Arms." A move was detected to disrupt the movement, but Ben Tillett kept the committee in continuous session, giving the traitors no opportunity to act ; they were swept along in the roaring rushing torrent of the battle.

Here, at the " Wades Arms," the helpers came along. John Burns' wife and Eleanore Marx-Aveling acted as correspondents for the committee ; they worked long hours and walked bravely late at night, or in the early morning, to and from their distant homes. Sacrifices unnoticed and numberless were made by nameless and known people, but all distinction was lost in this great inspiriting phase of the class struggle.

As the strike proceeded the claims of the strikers were formulated—8d. per hour by day and 1s. per hour by night ; regular calls at stated times and places ; the abolition of the sub-contract and piecework and the " plus " or bonus system. During the mediation that finally resulted in the end of the strike the demands changed to 6d. per hour, regular calls, access to accounts in all " plus " system work. These were practically the terms on which the strike was eventually settled.

Several thousands of the members of my union were thrown out of employment by the strike. None of them was entitled to lock-out pay as the union had not been in existence for six months, and one of the rules of the union was : " No member is eligible for benefit until he has paid twenty-seven weekly contributions." There was only one union, the Stevedores, that did pay strike pay, but their funds were soon exhausted.

The public supported the strikers and their hungry families. Over £50,000 was collected in various ways. Grants from trade unions—we gave £50—street collections, subscriptions, and all ways of keeping the thousands of men, women and children from starvation, were brought into use. From as far afield as Australia a sum of over £6,000 was cabled by the trades unions. The strike lasted six weeks. The Lord Mayor of London, the Bishop of London, Cardinal Manning and several other prominent people took part in negotiations to bring about peace. All this time the strikers' numbers increased ; blacklegs were brought into the dispute, but were of no value ; fights took place, and a few men were arrested. I got into a fight at Custom House, but suffered no great injury. Finally, Cardinal Manning was able to bring an end to the strike, under which the " docker's tanner " and nearly all their other claims were secured.

It was a great fight. One of the greatest in the history of the working-class in Great Britain. It ended once and for all the inhuman conditions under which the dockers had been compelled to work. It ended much suffering and misery in East End homes, and brought into being a great trade union of dock, wharf, riverside and transport workers, that has since, under the capable leadership of Ben Tillett, been able to protect the interests of thousands of workers who comprise its membership, and to improve their standard of living.

During the strike I met many people who have since loomed large in the public eye—George Lansbury, always an ardent worker for the down-trodden, H. H. Champion, members of the Bar, the Church, the Press, and other prominent people in other walks of life. It was a great and thrilling period for any one to live in ; it was still greater to be part of, and in the thick of, the struggle.

The developments in London were having repercussions in other parts of the country. Just after the settlement of the dockers' strike I received a letter from a gas worker in Bristol, named W. Vickery—he was acting on behalf of the gas workers there, who wanted to form a branch of the union. A branch was formed in September and I was called down to Bristol to deal with a situation that had arisen there. A big agitation had been going on at the three works in Bristol to secure the eight-hour day : the hours were twelve per day and the conditions very bad. A gang of stokers had to draw and charge twenty-five retorts per day, seven days a week, for a wage of 30s. These men wanted an increase of 5s. per week. The coal wheelers, who were getting 23s. 4d. per week, wanted an advance to 28s. per week. Worst of all were the labourers, who only received 17s. 9d. per week, for which they had to work from 6 a.m. to 5.30 for the first five days of the week, and then from 6 a.m. to 2 p.m. on Saturdays. These men wanted a wage of 21s. per week and the eight-hour day. The chief engineer said he would grant the advances if the men would draw and charge an extra five retorts per shift, an impossible task. The engineer was obdurate, in fact he was spoiling for a fight. No progress could be made. On Tuesday, October 6th, the first shift of men were paid off, and the next day the men at all three gas works came out on strike. The works were picketed, blacklegs were brought in. The pickets saw one lot, spoke to them, and they went home. One man came in a cab with his bag, a sailor ; we told him that trouble was on and he went away. We had a way of telling them. The pickets who were doing scout duty reported that a number of blacklegs were coming along Coronation Road, on their way to the Cannons Marsh works. A big crowd waited for them on College Green, but the blacklegs turned off in another direction. They were in brakes. The first load eluded the crowd, but the second brake load was stopped. " Free labour," as it was called, was taken in cabs to other works. This did not please the strikers and their many friends. Hundreds of people turned out, and brakes and cabs were overturned, and several of the strike-breakers were thrown into the river. Many fights took place near the works, and several of our men were prosecuted. At one of the works a brake load of men only got in with the aid of a detachment of fifty policemen. The police, knowing the conditions the men worked under, were fairly sympathetic. One of the officials had his topper hat knocked in ; he offered £10 reward to any one who would tell who did it, but he could not find out. Despite the introduction of a few blacklegs to break the strike, our efforts to hold up the works were effective. The men's leaders were sent for and were told that the directors were prepared to concede the men's claims ; the blacklegs were to be cleared out of the works, and none of the strikers were to be victimised. The big gasometers were very low and nearly empty, which meant that the town would soon be in darkness, and only then did the directors realise the value of the workers' labour.

The men resumed work the same day as the settlement, and by the time the night shift came on duty the retorts were charged and the works in full blast. During the strike a marquee had been erected in the works for the accommodation of the strike-breakers. Large quantities of meat, beer, tobacco, and different food had been brought in. The strikers, when they resumed work, made short work of what was left. This was the second important eight-hour day victory of the gas workers that had only become possible by organisation, backed up with unity and determination.

At last the Great Dock Strike was over. To the formation of a dockers' union the leaders of the strike then turned their attention. Ben Tillett and Tom Mann, who had helped me form my Gas Workers'

Union, undertook this task, helped by several well-known Labour leaders of the time. Ben Tillett became the general secretary, and Tom Mann the general president.

The formation of the Dockers' Union led to certain complications, and a little friction between their union and ours. Our principle was contained in our motto: " One Man, one Ticket, and Every Man with a Ticket." This in short meant that as long as a man or a woman had a trade union ticket they should be allowed to work side by side, in factories, workshops, at the docks, or anywhere else without any interference from any other trade union. Our object was to secure the consolidation of the trade union and Labour forces ; we wanted to eradicate quarrels between the workers because they belonged to different organisations, and realise the unity and oneness of the working class.

To this ideal, opposition immediately came from both Tom Mann and Ben Tillett. They wanted to put a " ring fence " around the docks and allow only the employment in the docks of members of the Dockers' Union, in a similar way to which the stevedores protected their preserves. I was strongly opposed to this policy, because, years before either my union or the Dockers' Union had been formed, it was the custom and practice of many of the dockers to work in the gas works during the winter when dock work was slack, and for the gas workers to work in the docks in the summer time when work was not so plentiful in the gas works.

If the formation of trade unions was going to enforce the hardship of unemployment on the workers, unless they belonged to more than one union, I knew that the cause of trade unionism would suffer. I was certain that the Dockers' Union policy would fail, because of so many general labourers being unemployed from time to time, and because such a system would intensify the inhuman competition for employment.

A great deal of friction was caused by the enforcement of this policy of the Dockers; several times it almost led to strikes at the Beckton, Poplar, Wapping, Stepney and Rotherhithe gas works, because our members took the view that if the Dockers' Union would not recognise our ticket, they would not recognise theirs. This policy was finally abandoned by the Dockers. I remember Tom Mann addressing a big mass meeting at the Canning Town Public Hall on his return from Australia. He said that "the time is now ripe to enforce the policy advocated by Thorne, that trade unions all over the country should recognise each other's tickets; men should work side by side and create real solidarity and comradeship." This started the abolition of the practice of poaching men away from different organisations. The workers were getting sick and tired of having to transfer from one union to another and then back again, paying fresh entrance fees each time, and in some cases after paying for benevolent benefit into one union the benefit would be lost on the transfer. Many of our best and most enthusiastic members had to join the Dockers' Union, whereas we had a rule that exempted members from other unions joining us.

Towards the end of 1889 the spirit of the "New Unionism" was flaming across the country, here, there and everywhere. Workers were rising for improvements in their wages and conditions; often unorganised, downtrodden, they took action without planning ahead; sheer desperation drove them to striking revolt, and with their striking came organisation.

In this way a big strike broke out at a gutta-percha and rubber works in Silvertown. The workers were not members of any union; later they joined my union. They struck work as one person, both men and women; their demand was for an increase in wages from $4\frac{3}{4}d.$ per hour to 6d. per hour for the yard labourers—"the docker's tanner." This was granted on the third day of the strike, but after the workers resumed work a "round robin," signed by every employee of the firm, was sent to the management demanding a general increase for every one. The management refused to grant this increase, and threatened to withdraw the increase granted to the yard labourers; this precipitated a general strike again of the whole works.

The strike continued. Meetings were held—we had lots of help from different speakers. One Monday morning while I was addressing a meeting of the strikers a bosom friend of mine arrived on the scene—this was the one and only Pete Curran. I feel that this story would be incomplete without a word or two about Pete. He was an active worker in the Labour movement, at first in different parts of Scotland. Coming to London he continued his propaganda work in a most vigorous fashion. Often he suffered victimisation, and was on the employers' "black list." He obtained work at the Woolwich Arsenal and joined my union, and was working there when the Silvertown Rubber Works strike started. He was driving a steam hammer on the night shift at the time, and after his shift, before going home, he would come and speak for me at the strike meetings. From this time on our friendship became very close and intimate, only ending with his death twenty years later. We had some trouble at the Arsenal over an alteration of working conditions. We called a protest meeting of the men; Curran was there—he came straight from work to address the meeting—the perspiration of toil was streaming from his face as he lashed out, defending the rights and privileges of the workers. He was victimised from the Arsenal over this dispute and became an official of the union. He did organising work; how effective he was at this work was illustrated on an organising tour in Ireland. A big trade union demonstration in Londonderry was fixed up by Pete one Saturday afternoon; over 10,000 people were in it and a procession was formed. Religious differences were very keen in those days, but when the procession swung into line the Catholic drum-and-fife band led the Protestants and the Protestant band led the Catholics ; so powerful was Curran that he had united these two differing sects on the common trade union platform.

Curran became the district secretary of the union for the West of England, with headquarters at Plymouth.

An employer at Plymouth Quay insisted on employing a certain number of non-union men. Curran warned him that unless he employed only union men he would " strike " the job. The employer declared it was " intimidation," and instituted proceedings against Curran under the conspiracy laws.

Curran was taken up at Plymouth Police Court, and I was present. Curran defended himself, and I have never heard a more splendid defence, not only of an individual, but of the principles of trade unionism and the rights of the workers. Notwithstanding this, he was sentenced to six weeks' imprisonment without the option of a fine.

The sentence created a sensation in the trade union world. Curran appealed, and the matter was taken up by the London Trades Council and the Parliamentary Committee of the Trade Union Congress. The best legal advice and assistance were secured for Curran, and the appeal was heard by Judge Bompas, Q.C. The judgment was upheld.

This decision was of the greatest importance to the trade unions of the country. It meant that, if the decision given in the police court and upheld by the learned judge was the correct interpretation of the law of the land, the workers were deprived of their greatest weapon, " the right to strike."

The case was taken to the High Court, and heard by the Lord Chief Justice, the late Lord Coleridge, and four other judges. After long legal discussion, it was found that the previous decisions could not be sustained. They were reversed and the conviction quashed. This was an historic event in trade union history, for if this victory had not been won no trade union official would

have been safe to discuss trade union matters or wages
and working conditions with an employer, and the
workers would have been robbed of their rights as free-
born citizens to withdraw their labour. The workers of
this country owe a deep debt to Curran on this account,
for, although he received united assistance, it was his keen
perceptive brain that saw the implication of the sentence
—a most dangerous precedent. Until his death Curran
continued to be an organiser of the union. He had many
qualities, but he excelled as a public speaker—eloquent,
witty, sometimes sarcastic, and capable of delivering
sledgehammer attacks of logic. He was always bright
and cheerful ; his sense of honour would not allow him
to criticise or denounce an opponent except in his
presence, and then he was fearless, caring not whether
he offended or pleased.

I was with Curran when he joined the Social Democratic Federation in the days of its inception, a time
when the principles of Socialism could only be ex-
pounded at great personal risk, but Curran's persuasive
powers won many converts. We fought together many
times in different causes.

Curran's election to Parliament as Member for the
Jarrow Division, in addition to being a very significant
event in the growth and development of the political
Labour Movement, was a most interesting public event.
Including Curran, there were six candidates : Curran for
Labour ; Alderman Callaghan, an Irish candidate ; Sir
Patrick Rose-Innes, a Tory ; Spencer Leigh Hughes
(" Sub Rosa " of literary fame), Liberal ; " Trousers "
Hannable, an Independent ; and another " freak "
candidate. Curran was elected, but the newspapers
featured " Trousers " Hannable, who did not go
to the poll because he could not obtain the deposit
money.

He had earned the nickname of " Trousers " at
Ilford, where he worked as a printer, and where he had
run for Parliament. During this contest he was
mobbed, and lost his nether garments. The name stuck

to him, and so did the residents of Jarrow, for, although he had retired from the contest, they would not let him leave the town. The people liked him for his humorous ways and his frankness, and until the election was over he was always followed by a self-constituted body-guard, who would not let him get back to his home in the south !

Curran made a big impression on the House of Commons in his brief membership of that body. His speeches were brilliant. Friends and opponents alike admired him, and Mr. Asquith, then Prime Minister, congratulated him on one occasion for the excellent way in which he had presented his case. Curran did fine work on different committees of the House of Commons, especially on the one appointed to inquire into the use of military force in an industrial dispute in Belfast. His defeat in 1910 was a great loss both to Labour and the House of Commons.

Curran distinguished himself, as the representative of British trade unionism, as a delegate to the American Federation of Labour, as Chairman of the General Federation of Trade Unions, and on the executive committees of both the National Labour Party and the Independent Labour Party. He was often a delegate to International Labour and Socialist congresses, and presided at one of the biennial congresses of my union.

I hope my readers will forgive me for halting my story to pay tribute to this old and very dear friend of mine, a man with whom I was intimately associated with in both my union and political work, and a man who on his death, shortly after his defeat at Jarrow in 1910, was buried with the highest honours that can be conferred on a member of the Labour Movement. His funeral was made the occasion of a huge gathering of friends and sympathisers from all parts of Great Britain and the Continent.

The Silvertown strike continued. We held on and kept up our meetings. One of the speakers at these meetings was a man named Michael Henry, a journalist, novel writer, and a smart platform orator ; he had just formed a union of coal porters. In one of his speeches he called the manager of the rubber works a "dirty dog." The manager heard of this, and declared that not one of the strikers would be allowed to return to work except on the manager's terms. Collections were made for the strikers, and although they were not entitled to any benefit from the union, we granted them £150. Eleanore Marx-Aveling took a leading part in the strike. An eloquent speaker, fluent in several languages, she did good service both among the men and women, and formed a women's branch of the union at Silvertown, of which she became the secretary. She sat as a delegate from this branch at all our delegate meetings, and was elected to the committee of the union when the rules were altered to permit women to be seated on the committee.

During the progress of the strike we were learning the need of greater and more efficient trade union machinery and organisation. I suggested to Michael Henry that it would be of great assistance to the workers if a federation was formed of his union of Coal Porters, my own union and the Miners' Federation. I thought that as a result of the enthusiasm that had been created by the formation of our union, and the development of trade unionism all over the country, the formation of such a federation would be possible. We told the Silvertown strikers and the gas workers of the country of our desire and intentions, explaining that with such an organisation, if a strike took place at any gas works, the coal miners at the pits would be able to prevent coal being sent to the gas works in dispute, and even if the miners could not do this effectively the coal porters could. We were all very keen about the project, but we soon found that the Miners' Federation were not yet prepared to form such an alliance. Michael Henry ceased to be the general secretary of the coal porters, and was succeeded by a big Irishman, Jim Connor.

Under his leadership the coal porters became federated to the Miners' Federation.

After lingering on for some time the Silvertown strike fizzled out, the strikers had to accept the manager's terms, many of the workers were victimised, left " on the stones," and had to seek employment elsewhere.

CHAPTER VI

THE turmoil of the various strikes having subsided, another awkward problem presented itself to me : to make up the accounts of the union.

The general secretary of a trade union is legally responsible for the keeping of the books of accounts and the proper spending of the funds. To carry on this part of my duties at the time I refer to caused me considerable anxiety.

Since the beginning of the union my time had been more than occupied with organising work, interviewing employers, dealing with disputes and general industrial affairs. It had been quite impossible for me to attend to financial matters, except merely to record the items of income and expenditure.

The union rules required me to submit to the Executive Council our first balance sheet for the half-year ending September, 1889. At that time we had between 15,000 and 20,000 members in over forty branches, each branch sending weekly its cash to the head office, together with the details of any moneys spent. The branches also sent a return for the half-year showing the amount remitted to me and what had been paid for benefits and local charges. These returns I had to check with my own records to ensure accuracy, and, as in numerous instances there were queries and differences between my records and those of the branch secretaries which had to be settled satisfactorily, it was a difficult job.

In addition to this I had a multitude of correspondence, vouchers, bills, etc., which were simply strewn everywhere about the office. There was no regular system of filing of any kind.

I must confess that account keeping and preparing balance sheets were tasks for which I had had no training or experience. But the job had to be accomplished somehow. I began by gathering up all papers I could find in the office and sorting them out into a semblance of order. An income of over £3,000 had to be accounted for. There were bills of every imaginable shape and size, written on all kinds of paper, in pencil and ink, a large proportion of them almost undecipherable. Our office then was just one small room, with meagre and primitive furniture, where the whole of our work had to be done, including the holding of committee meetings.

I shall never forget the sight of this room, simply covered as it was in all directions with those papers. It is inexplicable to me how I ever managed to get things together, but I did. I realised that unless I was ready with the accounts for the auditors at the appointed time the confidence of the members would be seriously shaken.

I worked two consecutive periods of a whole day and a night, with a two-day break only to devote to other duties.

At last a balance sheet emerged from the chaos, and to my intense relief the statement I prepared was duly audited and found correct. A copy is still in existence.

The experience I acquired on this job was not forgotten. I determined not to go on with the union work for the future unless I was given some competent help to deal with clerical office matters. I saw that no man living, no matter how industrious or capable he was, could hope satisfactorily to perform work which required personal attention both during the day and evening, at home and away from the office, sometimes involving travelling for days together.

In passing I may mention that to-day the account keeping at the head office of a large trade union, with its considerable income and **expenditure**, varying contributions and benefits, State insurance, legal department, and other sections, is a complicated and onerous business which places a great responsibility upon the shoulders of a general secretary, who has to be extremely careful to see that all this work is efficiently carried out by competent assistants appointed for the purpose. Very exacting requirements of the Registrar of Friendly Societies have to be met to ensure the safeguarding of the funds in the interests of the members.

With the balance sheet and statement of the accounts of the union I had also to render a general statement of my stewardship and the general position of the union. In this " First Half-Yearly Statement and Report " I congratulated the union on its financial position. I explained the difficulties that had been encountered as the result of both the inexperience of the branch secretaries and myself in the art of book-keeping and the framing of reports. I then dealt with the successful formation of the union after two or three futile attempts, and gave as my opinion for previous failures the fact that too much power had been vested in the delegates, who acted without consultation with the general body of the organisation, and also because the members did not take sufficient interest in their own welfare. I appealed for a still greater interest to be taken in the general Labour Movement.

" The majority of the members," I stated in my report, " are under the impression that, after visiting the club room and paying their subscriptions, that their duties are terminated. This is not so. How can you expect your leaders to fight your battles ? Each and every man must take his share of the work that has to be accomplished. We are a great organisation, with a great amount of work before us, to which each must contribute his share. Act to each as true brethren and sink all petty jealousies and frivolous charges, keeping the one grand thing—the union and the Labour Movement—in view."

I told them that sacrifices would have to be made if

they wanted their conditions of life altered, and showed them what had been accomplished already with the small contribution of 2d. per week.

" You are working the eight-hours day which has been so long looked for in all countries," I told them, " but was never adopted but in a few gas works in England, while at present every gas works in and around London for miles are working under the eight-hours system, and you, brother members, have been the means of finding some thousands of your fellow workmen employment, who would otherwise have been in a starving condition. And even though nothing more should be done, you will have the satisfaction of knowing that this has been brought about by your exertions.

" Then, again, look at the provinces, Manchester, Salford, Halifax, Bury, Shields, Sunderland, and the glorious victory which our Bristol comrades gained as another evidence of what can be done by combination. Likewise the many other kinds of labour which have improved their conditions by this union.

" The gas workers of England have shown the workers of the world a grand example, and it must be admitted that our union stimulated the minds of the dockers. Were not the whole of the working classes of the kingdom looking on while the gas stokers were agitating for the eight hours ? And I challenge any workmen to show where any of the working classes demonstrated in the same manner as the gas stokers.

" We are at present one of the strongest Labour unions in England. It is true we have only one benefit attached, and that is strike pay. I do not believe in having sick pay, out of work pay, and a number of other pays. We desire to prevent so much sickness and men being out of work. The way to accomplish this is, firstly, to organise ; then reduce your hours of labour or work—that will prevent illness and members being out of employment. The whole aim and intentions of this union is to reduce the hours of labour and reduce Sunday work. It can be dispensed with.

"We have been victorious. In every instance our demands have been acceded to except at Silvertown, which has been out on strike eight weeks at the time I write. We have granted them £150, to the dock labourers £50, and to Shoeburyness £25. This is sufficient evidence of what combination will effect, and we may congratulate ourselves upon the manner in which this union is being carried on.

"It must be admitted that all our branch secretaries knew nothing concerning book-keeping nor making out balance sheets; and when you placed me in the position of general secretary I was quite ignorant of these matters, and I acknowledge that I require a great amount of education on these points in common with the branch secretaries.

"You will perceive by the balance sheet that the expenses have been heavy, but if you take into consideration the number of branches which have been opened, the number of members who have joined, and the fact that each branch that is opened required a set of books, the cost of which is 23s., besides small books and other incidental expenses, the expenditure cannot be considered excessive.

"In conclusion, I hope that every member, male and female, will do their utmost to make our union one of the strongest in England, and I am glad that we have the females with us, it being our duty to help our fellow-women, and raise them from the starving position in which they are at present placed.

"Trusting that I may continue to enjoy the confidence of all my fellow-members in the future which I have hitherto had in the past,

"I remain,
"Yours faithfully.
"WILLIAM THORNE,
"*General Secretary.*"

That was my first report, of which I was justly proud. Since that report I have made many more, and in them is traced the gradual growth of our organisation to a strength of over one million workers during the latter war period, and its decline to its still substantial strength of over a half million workers of both sexes of many grades and categories.

The pause to prepare and present the balance sheet did not last long. The union was soon again involved in another dispute, this time at Bristol, where the dockers were on strike for an improvement in their wages. Many of the members of my union were on strike with them.

I visited the dockers' headquarters in Bristol and found my old friend, Tom McCarthy, in charge and leading the strikers. He told me that there was to be a big strike meeting at the Hay Market on the Friday night and asked me to come along and speak to the strikers. I said I would.

McCarthy told me that the dockers intended marching through the city, although they had been forbidden to do so by the superintendent of police. They carried out their intention and swung along through the city until they reached the bottom of Bridge Street; here they were met by both mounted and foot police.

A skirmish followed the meeting; the procession was broken up, to be quickly re-formed; a detour was then made by way of Bath Street to Castle Ditch, where the police were again encountered. After further deploying we all managed to get to the Hay Market and hold the meeting. As the meeting was proceeding the sheriff sent for the military and the Mayor arrived on the scene.

We finished the meeting and dispersed, but the military and police were both annoyed at being out-witted!

They harried and hurried the men as they moved off in little groups. This started some trouble, and the Lancers and the police charged the crowd. Many were hurt and arrested. I managed to get clear. The charge and the arrests did not satisfy the police, for during the night they continued their persecution by visiting the houses of dockers, taking them from their beds and placing them under arrest. Many of the dockers received six weeks' imprisonment over the affair. There are many of the men that fought in this dispute still alive. While in Bristol recently I met one of our members who proudly showed me his thirty-five union cards, one for each year since the formation of the organisation.

No labour leader or trade union official has ever worked harder than I did in those troublesome and strenuous days towards the end of 1889. The whole country was seething with discontent, and the wealth-producing workers up and down the country were striking to improve their wages and conditions, often without authority from their union, and in many cases not members of a trade union at all.

The strikers often asked me for advice, and I always pleaded with them to press for the eight-hour working day. In those days the general workers' hours of labour ranged from fifty and sixty-four hours per week to as many as seventy and eighty hours per week.

In nearly every case of a strike or a dispute the men and women concerned were successful; this was no doubt due to the union's success and the victory of the dockers in their fight for the " tanner " per hour. There were at least fifty strikes in progress at the end of 1889, and as a result of them millions of pounds were gained in wages, hours were shortened, and thousands of unemployed men and women were absorbed into industries. The employers had been taken by surprise and did not expect such a solid and virile development of trade unionism. It was a golden harvest and a real opportunity for the wage slaves.

We were opening branches in Ireland at this time, where, in many respects, the workers were in advance of their fellows in England. They had a federation of agricultural labourers, general workers and skilled artisans. This form of organisation was very strong in the south of Ireland, and when a strike took place employers were unable to secure " blacklegs," or " free labour " as it was sometimes called.

While on an organising tour in the north of Scotland I visited Dundee, where the Trade Union Congress was being held in the Gilfillan Memorial Hall. Being interested in the Trade Union Movement, and as our organisation had not yet affiliated to Congress, I was made a visitor for three days. At Congress I met George Shipton, the secretary to the London Trades Council, the largest in the country ; and also Henry Broadhurst, who was a member of Parliament and also secretary of the Trade Union Congress Parliamentary Committee.

It was an exciting Congress, and fiery scenes took place as a result of a resolution brought forward by Keir Hardie. In his resolution he made serious charges against Henry Broadhurst, alleging that he was a shareholder in the firm of Brunner, Mond & Co., and that at the recent elections he had supported sweaters and unfair employers of labour. The object of the resolution was to remove Broadhurst from the secretaryship of the Congress. John Wilson moved an amendment to Hardie's resolution expressing confidence in Broadhurst. The debate went on for two days and charges were hurled across the floor of Congress. Keir Hardie was accused of having had a newspaper that he was connected with printed at a non-union house. Hardie was able to refute these charges, but his resolution was lost by 177 votes to 11.

At this time the trade unionists were very bitter against Keir Hardie because at the previous Congress he had threatened to form an independent labour party. The idea was very distasteful to the so-called Labour Members in Parliament, who were really dominated by the Liberal Party.

Rather an amazing thing happened at this Congress

on the question of the eight-hour day. My union had secured it for its members, and yet a ballot of the unions affiliated to the Congress had turned down the eight-hour day by 62,883 votes to 39,629, although they voted in favour of trying to secure the eight-hour day through an Act of Parliament and in favour of a legal eight-hour working day for the miners. It occurred to me, after hearing these decisions, that the delegates were very inconsistent and reactionary.

From one end of the country to the other the gas workers were following the lead of London in demanding and securing both the eight-hour day and improvement in their wages. The South Metropolitan Gas Company in London, however, was one of the last to concede the eight hours. The eight-hour agitation was hardly over when I began a new agitation for the abolition of Sunday work, or the payment of double time when work was performed on Sunday. I explained to the men their right to have some time for leisure and pleasure, that this reform that I was after would give them the opportunity to visit their friends at the week-ends—something they were then unable to do—as well as being the means of absorbing many of the labourers into the iron works, brick yards, and other industries. I knew that the employers that I would have to meet in connection with this demand could not plead foreign competition as an excuse for refusing to grant double time for Sunday or its entire abolition. The Press got to know about this demand for double time for Sunday work, and the accounts they printed were not very encouraging. One newspaper described me as an " infatuated donkey." They declared that the cost of the shorter working day that we had secured, and the double pay for Sunday work that we wanted, like all good things, must be paid for. The cost, they said, must either come out of interest, capital profit, or wages, and if capital and interest were to be reduced there would be less motive to save, because people only saved with the object of getting interest on their capital.

The men were very enthusiastic about the demand, and finally a delegate meeting was held, at which I was instructed to petition the gas companies " for double time for Sunday between the hours of 6 a.m. and 10 p.m." To make this demand was not in accordance with the rules of the union, which laid down that one of the objects of the union was to secure double pay for Sunday work between the hours of 6 a.m. and 6 p.m. As general secretary, I had to remind the delegates about this rule. I told them that this new demand, coming so quickly after the eight-hour day had been granted, would be prejudicial. I was convinced that the directors of the gas companies would be annoyed at this new demand, but it was finally agreed that the demand should be for double time between the hours of 6 a.m. and 10 p.m. on Sunday. We met the representatives of all the London Metropolitan Gas Companies at the Cannon Street Hotel, where the claim was placed before the employers. After long arguments, the employers told us they could not grant our full demand, but that they were prepared to recommend the directors to pay double pay for the period from 6 a.m. to 6 p.m., but not for the extra four hours. I told them that I did not think the men would accept anything that the employers had put forward. I told them we were not prepared to ratify anything except double pay from 6 a.m. to 10 p.m. without consulting the members, and that we would take their suggestions and place them before the men, and meet the employers again. Following the meeting with the employers, we held a number of public and delegate meetings in different parts of the country for the purpose of discussing the employers' offer. At every meeting a resolution was passed unanimously instructing me not to compromise in any shape or form, but to insist upon double pay between the hours of 6 a.m. and 10 p.m.

From the beginning of my union's formation employers in all parts of the country were becoming apprehensive of its strength and its success. The trade and other papers attacked us for attempting to interfere, as they said, with the employers' business and " managerial functions." It was stated that there was no necessity for a trade union for the gas workers now that the eight-hour day had been secured, and they prophesied that the workers would soon realise this, and that the union would collapse. The employers did not content themselves with these appeals to the men to leave the union, but other methods were adopted.

A bonus scheme was introduced under which the men would receive one per cent. on their year's wages for every penny reduction below 2s. 8d. per 1,000 cubic feet of gas. The money that would accumulate, however, could not be withdrawn by the men except in case of death, and would earn an interest of 4 per cent. The workers had to sign an individual agreement that they would remain sober, that they would serve in any capacity in the gas works for a period of twelve months, and agree to obey the orders of the foreman.

The bonus scheme—or " bogus scheme," as I called it—was a direct attempt to smash the union. One of the clauses in it debarred the men from receiving the bonus if they participated in a strike. Many of the gas workers accepted the bonus scheme, and Mr. Livesey, of the South Metropolitan Gas Company, was making great progress with it during the time we were discussing the employers' offer to our demands for double pay for Sunday work.

Trouble was brewing. The situation was developing rapidly, both because of the refusal of our claim and the introduction of the bonus scheme; and we heard that Mr. Livesey had organisers in different parts of the country taking names and addresses of men who were prepared to work in the gas works in case of the strike that he anticipated, an anticipation that was soon realised.

The negotiations on the question of payment of Sunday work continued. Branch meetings and mass meetings of the men were held in different parts of

London, all of which were unanimous in rejecting the company's offer.

In the midst of these negotiations, Mr. George Livesey launched his bonus scheme, which immediately became the issue between ourselves and the company. We demanded the withdrawal of this so-called profit-sharing scheme, but Mr. Livesey was obdurate. On behalf of over 2,000 of the men, I tendered strike notices unless this anti-trade union scheme was withdrawn. Measures were promptly taken by the company to secure " blacklegs " in the event of a strike, and the police intimated that they would give the company every assistance in maintaining order at the gas works.

A deadlock was reached, and the strike began on December 5th, 1889. Blacklegs were imported. Many of them had their meals and slept in the gas works. Those that did not were given 2s. 6d. a day in lieu of food. The men responded to the strike call ; offers of assistance came from various quarters. Michael Henry, of the Coal Porters' Union, brought his members out in sympathy. John Burns offered to help us.

The weather was bad, but great meetings were held in different parts of London, attended by two, three, and four thousand men. Processions were held and, headed by bands and banners, toured from the Old Kent Road—where our central strike committee were sitting—through Deptford, Rotherhithe, St. George's, Vauxhall, and other affected areas, and a considerable amount of money was collected *en route*. Other expedients were resorted to to raise money. On Christmas week I suggested to my Executive Council that, in addition to the strike pay, we should give the men an extra half-crown towards their Christmas dinner. The Council agreed to this, and Mr. Byford—carrying a leather bag containing the money for the strike pay and this extra half-crown—and I started out for the various strike committees on the south side of the river that were in the Old Kent Road, Vauxhall, Greenwich, and Rotherhithe. We had just passed the " Aberfeldy "

public-house when a rough, hefty-looking man came up
to us and asked for a match. As I was feeling in my
pockets for a match, he made a grab for the treasurer's
bag. My previous boxing experiences had taught me
how to defend myself, and I prevented the man from
getting the bag. As he started to run away, I tripped
him with my foot. He quickly regained his feet and
ran down Abbot's Road, with myself and Byford in
pursuit. I was blowing a police whistle as I went. In
a moment a policeman was on the scene. I explained
what had happened, but that was the beginning and
end of the incident.

As the strike continued, sympathisers with us came
from unexpected quarters. A city tea merchant, Mr.
C. J. Rowe, presented us with a large chest of Indian
tea. We sold the tea at the usual price, and the money
went to the strike fund. Mr. Rowe continued to supply
tea to us, which, in addition to selling to the strikers,
we sold at the various branches. We found that this
led to trouble with some of the shopkeepers, who,
because the tea was not bought from them, refused to
sell our people sugar. But we soon got over this.

While the strike lasted the profits on the sale of tea
and sugar went to the strike fund, but afterwards we
accumulated the money, extended the business, and
sold other articles. Finally we opened a store in
Barking Road, Canning Town, near the head office of
the union. This store was a big success, and led to the
opening of a bakery. The bakery venture failed, but
another attempt to run a bakery was made.

Dick Mansfield and myself interviewed a wealthy
friend, who guaranteed the project to the extent of
£4,000. We obtained premises and got machinery.
Right from the start the venture was a success. The
£4,000 was paid back, and to-day we have six vans on
the road and are using as much as 2,000 sacks of flour
a week. Since the formation of the bakery big exten-
sions have been made to the plant, and the property
is valued at many thousands of pounds. The profits

from the bakery, although the bread is sold cheaper than at the ordinary bakeries, is used to subsidise our political efforts. Our nominees who are elected to the Town Council are paid the wages they lose while attending to their municipal duties. At general elections our candidates are made grants up to £300 towards their election expenses, and no less than fifty out of sixty-four candidates have been returned, either as councillors or Members of Parliament, with the assistance of the bakery. Mr. Ben Gardener, the present Mayor of West Ham, is one of our candidates who has received support from the bakery. For many years I have been pleased to serve as the honorary treasurer of this unique venture, known as "The Workers' Supply Association."

As the strike continued efforts were made by various people, including the local Members of Parliament, to bring about a settlement of the dispute. Finally, in the early part of February, 1890, and as a result of the intervention of the London Trades Council, of which George Shipton was the secretary, an agreement was arrived at. The agreement laid down that the company would revert to the eight-hour day. (During the strike they had gone back to the twelve-hour working day.) As vacancies occurred, the former workmen were to be given the opportunity of returning to their employment in preference to strangers. The company agreed to these terms and we recommended the men to accept them, which they did. A little while after this I was called to Plymouth for the purpose of organising the unskilled workers there, and at one of the big meetings which I addressed I explained the cause of the dispute in London. During my speech I said, " I would not think about giving a day's notice, much less fourteen days' notice, if I have to take charge of another similar dispute."

Mr. Livesey learnt of this remark from the newspapers, and made it an excuse for refusing to take back the strikers as he had agreed to. As a matter of fact,

very few of the old hands ever returned to the employ
of the South Metropolitan Gas Company. It was a
costly and unsuccessful strike, the union paying out
over £20,000 in strike pay and other expenditure. We
had the satisfaction, however, of knowing that it cost
the company in the neighbourhood of a quarter of a
million pounds.

During this big strike in London the union had lots
of other troubles. Employers all over the country were
counter-attacking against the conditions and concessions that we had gained following the formation of
the union. At Manchester and Salford trouble arose
over the employment of non-unionists.

The Manchester town clerk and the chairman and
members of the Gas Committee had large notices posted
inside the works offering better wages and conditions
to all men who would leave the union. This notice
caused a great deal of excitement. The men wanted to
down tools at once. In fact, notices were tendered to
the Gas Committee, but the district chairman of the
union refused to sign the notices, which, however, the
company accepted. I rushed to Manchester and sought
an interview with the Gas Committee, and asked them
to allow the notices to be withdrawn. They refused.
The Corporation posted notices, when the strike began,
explaining to the ratepayers the cause of the strike and
the short supply of gas. I at once sent for Picard, one
of our organisers, who had been victimised after the
London strike. He was a very active official and a
lucid platform speaker. Together we drew up a statement, and had it printed and posted, as a means of
counteracting the statements made by the Manchester
Corporation. Meetings of the men were held, and when
the Manchester men came on strike the men from
Salford stated that the gas mains from Salford had been
joined to the Manchester mains, and they also wanted
to strike for this reason.

I told the men that it was nonsense, and I also
received an assurance from the responsible people of the

PICTURE COURTESY GMB

The first known photograph of Will Thorne, as a young
gasworker and trade union activist, taken in the mid
to late 1880s.

PICTURE COURTESY J. CALLOW

Stokers charging the retorts with coal, at the Beckton gas-works, winter 1878. The hellish nature of the work, the sheer scale of the industrial enterprise, and the immense collective and physical effort required to feed the furnaces are clearly evident.

FACES OF LABOUR

PICTURE COURTESY GMB

The nature of industry: the Beckton Gasworks was almost a city in its own right; a sprawling 150-acre site, built out of the marshes, that provided London with its heat and light.

PICTURE COURTESY GMB

Two teams of Stepney gasworkers, photographed c. 1900, with the large scooped shovels and jagged lumps of coal that were the hallmarks of their industry.

SYMBOLS OF STRUGGLE

PICTURE COURTESY GMB

A delegate's card from the Congress of the Second Socialist International, organised by Will Thorne and held in London, in July 1896.

The Gasworkers' Union sponsored the Socialist Sunday School movement and campaigned for universal, secular, state education. This poster advertised a demonstration, in Ipswich, on 'Children's Sunday', 1909. Both these illustrations were by Walter Crane. The labour movement at this time prided itself in being at the forefront of developments in art and design.

PICTURE COURTESY GMB

PICTURE COURTESY GMB

Eleanor Marx: the union's first women's organiser. Will Thorne prized her bravery and intelligence, and her portrait was carried proudly by the gasworkers on the first May Day march, in 1890.

PICTURE COURTESY GMB

The earliest photograph of the Executive of the Gasworkers' Union, taken in the mid-1890s. This was a tight-knit and highly motivated group of men. Some have come straight from their workplaces to the photographer's studio, others have dressed up for the occasion. Prominent among them are:

Will Thorne (front row, centre); Mark Hutchins (front row, far right), the union's first President; Pete Curran (front row, fifth from left); and a young J.R. Clynes (second row, second left).

PICTURE COURTESY TUC

The Parliamentary Committee of the TUC, Bristol, 1898. The Colston Hall burned down during the congress, and Thorne is pictured (front row, first left) squatting amid the ruins. Mark Hutchins (middle row, fifth from right) and Pete Curran (back row, second right) also represent the Gasworkers. The contrast in style, fashion and formality between the delegates from the 'Old', skilled unions and those from the 'New', unskilled unions, was reflected, just as strongly, in their politics.

PICTURE COURTESY J. CALLOW

On the campaign trail: the Countess of Warwick urging voters to back Will Thorne, in West Ham, during the general election, January 1906. Thorne sits immediately behind her on the cart, with Curran to the right. Thorne was to take the seat for Labour with a majority of 5,237 votes over his Conservative opponent.

PICTURE COURTESY GMB

Constitutional politics: Labour MPs meeting, prior to the 1907 TUC Congress. Will Thorne, Richard Bell and William Steadman sit on the row nearest to the camera. All three had been instrumental in founding the Labour Party in 1900.

PICTURE COURTESY GMB

Revolutionary politics: Will Thorne, James O'Grady and
Stephen Sanders in Petrograd, 1917, as part of the British
Labour Delegation to Russia, after the February Revolution.
They flank the young soldier, with fixed bayonet, who persuaded the other men of the Volisnky regiment – gathered
around for the picture – to disobey the Tsar's orders to fire
upon the crowds.

PICTURE COURTESY GMB

Will Thorne on the eve of the Great War. He is shown here as a mature, capable and assured leader, who had already served as General Secretary for twenty-five years. He had another nineteen still to go. A volume of Tennyson's poems sits under his arm. Is it a studio prop? Or does it give the lie to the claims of J.R. Clynes that Thorne's 'reading passed by the poets ... and the classics', in favour of 'good magazines' and political journalism?

Salford Corporation that they had no intention of joining up the mains.

The Salford men were not satisfied, and came on strike, like the Manchester men, without union sanction. A meeting was held with the representatives of the Corporation, when it was found that the men had been misleading myself and my officials as to the facts of the dispute.

Manchester and Salford were like twin towns of a million candles. Shops, factories, and theatres were shut down. Churches and chapels were in darkness. It would have been amusing had it not been so tragic to realise what this primitive and fairy-like illumination meant to this big industrial centre.

John Burns, always happy in a fight, accepted the invitation of the men to go and speak to them. A meeting was held in Stevenson's Square on the Sunday afternoon. The square and the six streets leading into it were packed with people. I had never seen such a crowd before ! It is funny to recollect that, while John Burns was addressing this meeting in Manchester, his old colleague, Michael Henry, at one time secretary of the Coal Porters' Union, was in London denouncing " Mister Burns " with all the fluent vituperation of which he was capable !

Manchester Gas Committee, taking a leaf from the book of the South Metropolitan Company, had prepared for the strike.

As soon as the men came out on strike, blacklegs, or " nob-sticks," were marched in. The strikers and their supporters assembled in the adjacent streets with the intention of using other than peaceful persuasion with the blacklegs. The police, hearing of their intention, charged down the streets and cleared the crowd away.

I was in one of the side streets, but my previous experience in such affairs enabled me to avoid the consequences of the charge or of being locked up.

Inside the works, the men who had taken the strikers' places had a merry old time !

Only the other day I was talking to one of our old members, Tom Prince, who went through the strike. He told me that a canteen had been set up inside the works, and the men were given their meals and also a liberal supply of beer, tobacco, and other comforts.

This strike, like the dispute in London, was a failure. Hundreds of men who went on strike, both at Manchester and Salford, were never able to go back to work again for either of the two corporations. I thought, and still think, it was one of the most foolish strikes that the union was ever connected with.

The men went on strike without the authority of the union. Like the men at the South Metropolitan Gas Works, they were intoxicated with their own success ; they thought it was only necessary to threaten the employers to get whatever they asked for.

Many paid the penalty for this erroneous idea, and for disregarding the advice of myself and my Executive Council.

I warned the men that it was much more difficult to fight a corporation than a private employer, or even a big company, because in the case of a corporation it was the ratepayers' money that was being used, and not the private funds and profits of individuals.

It was several years before union men were again employed by the Manchester and Salford Corporation, but I am pleased to say that at the present time—and largely due to the efforts of Tom Prince—the workers there are very well organised.

It was just a little while after these two strikes that I met J. R. Clynes, now the Right Honourable J. R. Clynes, P.C., M.P., former Lord Privy Seal and ex-Minister of His Majesty's Government.

He was only twenty-one years of age at the time and was working as a piecer in a cotton mill. I soon found out that he was a very smart and intelligent young fellow ; in fact, he was much smarter than I was, although I was the general secretary of a large trade union organisation.

Clynes was taking an active interest in the Irish Home Rule Movement, and was one of the moving spirits of the trade union and political labour work of Oldham. He was approached by some of our members to start a branch of the Gas Workers' Union in the district where he lived. He accepted their invitation, joined the union and became the chairman of the branch, which very soon became very large and successful.

Clynes, through the chairmanship of the branch, had a lot to do with the Lancashire district of the union. He soon became the organiser to the district and later district secretary. Looking back over the balance sheets, I noticed in the one for the year ending March, 1892, this item :

" EXPENDITURE. MR. CLYNES.

"Away from home two nights . . . allowed 2s."

. At that time we paid our organisers only 30s. per week, and when away from home all day and all night 3s. 6d. was allowed.

I can assure my readers that Clynes and Picard (also a general organiser) had a very rough time, because it was impossible for them to have anything like a decent bed and food on this meagre allowance. Happily things have changed very much since those days, and both salaries and expenses are on a more adequate scale.

In those early days I am sure that neither I nor Clynes thought that he would become a Cabinet Minister, although I remember that after a speech which Clynes made at a public function I said to him : " Friend Clynes, you should be a Cabinet Minister ! "

Any one who knows or who has heard Mr. Clynes cannot but be impressed by his reasonable and thoughtful speech, and there are few orators more capable and convincing than he is.

He was only earning £1 a week when I first met him.

Many times we have talked over the hardships that we both endured in our young days. Much of Mr. Clynes' spare time in those far-off years was devoted to self-instruction. He is a voracious reader and a great lover of Shakespeare. I have heard him quote long passages without a fault from the works of the great poet.

Mr. Clynes became the president of our union many years ago, and he has rendered very valuable service, not alone to our organisation, but to the whole Trade Union Movement. During the whole thirty-six years that I have known him we have never had any cause to quarrel. His knowledge of the rules of debate make him an excellent chairman. Brilliant demonstrations of this ability have been seen at our Biennial Conference and at rank-and-file meetings at which he has presided.

On Christmas, 1918, he presented me with his book, " From Mill-boy to Minister," and it was inscribed : " In recollection of a long and valued friendship. To Thorne from Clynes, Xmas, 1918."

CHAPTER VII

FRIENDSHIP AND FIGHTS

BACK in London I was meeting all sorts and conditions of men. I remember meeting the present editor of the *Daily Mail*, Sir Thomas Marlowe, and Lord Dalziel, who has been connected with the ownership and management of several daily and weekly newspapers.

The first time I met these two gentlemen was at the " Democratic Club," in Chancery Lane, where they came in search of " copy." This was the home of the advanced school of economic and political thinkers of the time—the Radicals. Marlowe and Dalziel were what was known as " penny-a-liners," a term derived from the amount of compensation they used to receive from the newspapers to which they contributed as freelances. Many other people later to be well known in public life used to come to this club, among them the late Mr. Morrison Davidson, Cunninghame Graham, and all the Labour Leaders of the time.

Eventually the club was closed down and a new club started in Essex Street, off the Strand, where lesser and more peculiar people made rendezvous.

I doubt whether in those days either Marlowe or Dalziell ever expected to reach the great heights they have in politics and journalism, or to receive the fabulous salaries they do. Those days, those clubs, are both memories of the past.

Near to the Chancery Lane lived Eleanor Marx-Aveling and Dr. Aveling. I knew them well. It was Eleanor that helped me more than any one else to improve my very bad handwriting, my reading and general knowledge. One day they asked me to come along to their flat to meet the very young Jean Longuet, who later became a famous member of the French Senate and the able and devoted lieutenant of the great Jean Jaures. Longuet was the grandson of Karl Marx. I had first seen him when he was a baby, and often played with him and amused him, little realising that one day he would become a brilliant lawyer and a great workers' advocate, both in the French Parliament and in International working-class efforts.

It was during the big London dispute that I first met the Rev. William Morris. At that time he was the vicar of St. Anne's Church near Nine Elms Lane, where he used to deliver very democratic sermons, and often during the strike he spoke to the men at Vauxhall. Later he was elected a trustee of the union. For his courage and the expression of his love for humanity that shone through his writings and speeches he was unfrocked from the Church of England. This caused quite a stir amongst the strikers. I was at a meeting in Vauxhall when they first heard the news, and their annoyance was a tribute to the genuine service, both spiritual and material, that he had rendered, not alone to them, but to the workers generally. I believe it would have done the people good who were responsible for unfrocking him if they could have seen and heard the men. Morris used to be a great inspiration to the workers, especially when he lectured on art and industry. I often heard such lectures by him at Battersea, Victoria Park, and other places.

The late H. M. Hyndman was very active in these days, both as a writer and a speaker. He often spoke to the members of the Canning Town branch of the S.D.F. I was the chairman at one of the lectures that he gave on the subject of his book " England for All," and later he presented me with an autograph copy of the book. He had a happy way of stroking his long whiskers when he was talking, but this tonsorial adornment was not the only reason for him being regarded as the Father of Socialism. It was for his untiring work and the expounding and propagating socialistic and humanitarian ideas. He was always very optimistic in those days about the early consummation of the Social Revolution.

When Colonel John Ward became a member of the Battersea branch of the S.D.F. Hyndman paid special attention to him, as he believed he would become a big man in the Socialist movement. This was only one of Hyndman's minor mistakes. Jack Ward wrote some rather remarkable pamphlets in those days. I forget for the moment the titles, but I read them at the time. Ward, as well as being a member of the S.D.F., was also a member of the Battersea branch of my union, but he left both the union and the S.D.F. some years later. It always galls me to think that when a man belongs to an organisation in which he takes an active part that when he leaves it for no better reason than Ward did, that he should go out of his way to attack his late friends and their principles as he did. Ward could say nothing bad enough about the S.D.F., and, like John Burns, later on expressed himself in opposition to all the things that in former days he had been an adherent to. I sometimes think that such people only come into our movement for what personal aggrandisement they can get out of it. Hyndman was not of this type or calibre. He could have died a wealthy man, but he spent a life fortune in the Socialist movement, and very few people in this country have made the same financial sacrifice as he did during the forty or more years in which he took an active part in it.

While union work was making a great call upon my time I still found odd hours to give to the political and Socialist side, and in this way I accepted an invitation from the Canning Town branch of the S.D.F. to deliver a lecture to the members. The subject I chose was " Competition." The reason why I decided to speak upon this subject was my intimate association with the inhuman competition taking place in industry, and as I had endeavoured to minimise and smooth away the

friction of man pitted against man for a few hours'
work and a few pence in my agitation for the reduction
of hours of gas workers and other general labourers, I
thought the speech would be very appropriate. Will
Harris, the man who had sent me a telegram on the
Sunday before the big London dock strike, was my
chairman. I was very nervous. For days before the
lecture I thought and wondered whether the speech
would be a success, but on taking the platform my
nervousness disappeared and both my audience and
myself were well satisfied, and a good collection was
made.

The success of the gas workers and general labourers
had set other classes of workers thinking, and early in
1890 a deputation of shop assistants from Jones' Tea
Company in Poplar approached me, and asked if I
could do anything for them to improve their wages and
shorten their hours of labour. There was no " Shop
Hours Regulations Act " at that time. I investigated
their conditions, and after several meetings with the
shop assistants I was in a position to take up their case.
I wrote a letter to the manager of the firm at the head
office, in Crisp Street, Poplar. I had no reply. So I
wrote again, when the manager, in a rather annoyed
frame of mind, wanted to know what business it was of
mine to interfere with his assistants, and what did I
know about the work ? I admitted that I'd never
packed tea, or cut up bacon, or made pats of butter,
but I did know the hours of work were very long and
the pay very small. After one or two interviews the
manager made considerable improvements both in pay
and in hours of the assistants. He soon found out that
there was more profit in treating his staff well than
otherwise, and he became a very good employer of
labour. We became quite good friends, but he could
never understand why a man in corduroys should take
up the case of the black-coated workers instead of a
man wearing a long coat and top hat. The manager
and the assistants joined together and presented me

with a fine Malacca walking stick as a token of appreciation of what I had done for them. From this time on I took more than a passing interest in the conditions of shop assistants, and my efforts and agitation were, I think, without boasting, a great help and a jumping-off ground for the organisation of the present Shop Assistants' Union that to-day guards the interests of thousands of such workers.

These were only side lines, though; my own members needed more and more attention. There were new fields to conquer. The brickfields of Kent, Surrey and Essex claimed my attention, and I soon had them well organised within the union. The method of payment in those days was much different to what it is now. In some cases one man would undertake to do the work of moulding, drawing, setting, and burning the bricks by contract, and he would pay the men different rates. The men wheeling the bricks—fifty bricks on a barrow—received from ten to twelve shillings per day, and a pint of beer for each shilling. The payment for moulding bricks varied. The payment, however, was considered inadequate, and a demand was made for an increase in wages. The brickmasters refused to make any concessions. They sneered at the fact that the brick workers had joined the union, which they likened to a mushroom that had sprung up over night and which would die as quickly. The action of these employers precipitated a strike. Thousands of workers in the different fields came out. It was an expensive strike while it lasted, but we finally secured a good increase in wages amounting to about 4d. per thousand for the bricks made and handled. There were other strikes in the brickfields after this for a reduction of hours, the hours being from six in the morning to six at night, with a half-hour for breakfast and an hour for dinner; with two other spells, one at eleven o'clock and the other at four o'clock. These two spells, one in the morning and one in the afternoon, were known as "beer time." The men would drink two quarts of beer at each spell. The work necessitated such drinking, but my readers can see what an inroad was made in the wages at twelve shillings per day by the cost of this beverage. Happily this system does not exist to-day.

Beer played a prominent part in the industry in those days. In the gas works a man would come round the works with a barrel of beer. He was called the "Potty." He came round about eleven o'clock in the morning and about 3.30 in the afternoon selling beer to the men. This practice has also been done away with, and in most gas works oatmeal is supplied to the men during the hot weather.

Through all the early years I have described one main idea was firmly rooted in my mind. It was that by the reduction of hours that the conditions of the workers could best be improved. We had in several industries secured the eight-hour working day, but to secure it was not enough. I wanted it legalised.

My agitation was responsible for a delegate meeting being called in January, 1890, to consider the question of the legal eight-hour day. The conference declared in favour of the proposal, and authorised me to organise a demonstration to be held on Sunday, May 4th. I at once put myself in touch with Dr. Aveling, who was acting as secretary to the Bloomsbury Socialist Society, with a view to getting his assistance to organise a demonstration in Hyde Park. We decided to summon a delegate meeting. Invitations were sent to all labour organisations, trade unions and Radical clubs. Seventy-five delegates were present at the meeting, and opinion was unanimous in favour of demonstrating for the legal regulation of the working day. Certain details had to be arranged, and a further delegate meeting was called for Sunday, April 6th, at the Workmen's Club, Gye Street, Vauxhall. Rev. William Morris presided, and ninety-four organisations were represented. It was decided that Sunday, May 4th, would be the most suitable and practical date for the demonstration for all concerned. A central committee was appointed, of which I was one of the secretaries, and from then until the demonstration we were kept busy with the many details that had to be arranged. A manifesto was drawn up and 100,000 copies were printed and circulated. During the preliminary meetings Dr. Aveling called our attention to the fact that a resolution similar to that which we were demanding had been passed at an International Conference held in Paris, July 14th to 29th, 1889. I had been in touch with the secretary of the International, who informed me that at the conference 400 delegates, representing twenty-two countries, had discussed the legal limitation of the working day, day work, night work, and the supervision of women and child labour. I also learnt that similar demonstrations for the legal limitation of hours had been held in the United States, under the auspices of the American Federation of Labour.

There were fifteen platforms in Hyde Park for the demonstration. They were occupied by representatives of all the older trade unions and the London Trades Council. The latter body, while in favour of the eight-hour day, objected to the phrase " by legal enactment." Members of Parliament were present, and ,John Burns and Michael Davitt were on two of the platforms.

This demonstration was one of the largest ever held in Hyde Park. From Marble Arch all the way to Achilles statue was a solid mass of people. It was estimated by the newspapers the following day that at least 250,000 people were present, and great excitement and enthusiasm prevailed when the following resolution, that was put from every platform simultaneously, was carried with cheers and shouting :—

" That this mass meeting recognises that the establishment of an International Working Day of Eight Hours for all workers is the most immediate step towards the ultimate emancipation of the workers, and urges upon the Governments of all countries the necessity of fixing a working day of Eight Hours by legislative enactment."

That was many years ago ; but the workers have yet to win international legislation for the eight-hour day. It is pleasing to see that the recent work of the League of Nations brings the possibility of such legislation nearer.

The life of a trade union leader is full of shocks and surprises. One of these shocks was awaiting me when I went to my office one morning and found a very stern letter from the Registrar of Friendly Societies. The letter pointed out to me that I had infringed the law by not sending him the annual returns for the union. Various forms, showing detailed expenditure, must be filled in and sent from the union to the Registrar, and failing to do this makes a union and its general secretary liable to heavy penalties. After recovering from my shock, I at once started to work to knock the two half-yearly balance sheets into one in compliance with the regulations of the Registrar. This was no easy task. For about three weeks I struggled with my small knowledge of the art of figures, and when I finally finished the job I felt more fit for a lunatic asylum than to be a general secretary of a trade union. One of my great difficulties was in collating the branch balance sheet ; none of the branch secretaries had brought forward their balance sheets from the previous year, and I had to send them back to the branch secretaries several times. After I thought I was finished I found that I was twopence halfpenny out in my balance. For one whole day I searched for this twopence halfpenny. At last I thought everything was in order and off went the documents to the Registrar. Another shock was awaiting me—within two days my report came back again from the Registrar covered over with red ink marks. There were dozens of them, and each one meant a mistake. I got to work again, and, after much more labour, sent them corrected and in order to the Registrar, who this time was satisfied with my arithmetic.

I felt like having a holiday after nearly a month of brain-racking work that I was not used to ; but there was no holiday for me. The First Annual Conference, that was to be held at the Workmen's Club in Gye Street, Vauxhall, had to be prepared for. This meant more reports of income and expenditure, and a detailed account of the work of the union and its activities in strikes and lock-outs. There had been a great number of strikes and two lock-outs, and it was almost an impossibility to give a full and accurate report, but I did my best.

That very brave and intelligent woman, Mrs. Aveling, was the secretary to the Conference and made the work smoother for all concerned.

Delegates were present at the Conference from England, Scotland, Ireland and Wales, and the chief business was to frame a new code of rules, the union's experience having shown us that many amendments were necessary to our first set of rules.

I apologised to the Conference for the lack of detail in my report, and explained to them that the treasurer, the assistant secretary and myself had been doing our best in the midst of most difficult circumstances to supply them with all the information they would require. The union was only a year old, but it had been in more strikes and struggles in that year than any other union in existence at the time. The threat of Mr. Livesey, made during the big London strike, to smash the union had failed, and the union was steadily going stronger, despite the fact that employers in every part of the country were harassing us. Where other unions were tolerated, we were being attacked. Our most active members were being victimised, but we were not downhearted.

I have in front of me as I write a photograph of the delegates of the First Annaul Conference. There are few of them still alive, but they were all a brave, determined lot, and they laid well the foundations upon which the present greatness of the union has been built.

The new rules were drafted and accepted by the Conference. As a preamble to them I stated that trade unionism had done excellent work in the past, and that it was the hope of the workers for the future. It must recognise that there are only two classes, the working class and the possessing master class, and that these two classes have nothing in common.

I felt very proud as I stood before that Conference and told the delegates that the immediate objects of the union were to improve the material conditions of its members; the raising of their status from mere beasts of burden to human beings; to make brighter and happier the home of every worker; the saving of little children from the degrading, hard and bitter lot to which many of them were condemned; a more equitable division amongst all men and women of the tears and laughter, the joys and sorrows, and the labour and leisure of the world. I told the delegates that if they kept these aims clearly before them they would march steadily and irresistibly towards the emancipation of the working class.

There is no doubt that my advice was heeded in a practical way by everybody in the union. It made the organisation most democratic, and, above all, a fighting organisation; the only benefits we paid were strike and lock-out pay and legal protection. I did not believe in funeral benefits and in making the union a burial society. I believed that if we spent most of our union money on burying our members it would not be possible to improve the material conditions of the living. In this the union was unique, as being the only organisation not encumbered by all sorts of benevolent benefits.

After reporting to the Conference about the successful issue of a strike with the Norwich Gas Company, a Mr. Watkinson was elected president of the union, Mr.

Byford was re-elected treasurer, I was confirmed in my position as general secretary, and the Rev. William Morris was elected as one of the trustees of the union. Delegates were also appointed to attend the next year's Trade Union Congress. I was, of course, one of the delegates. I was instructed to prepare a scheme for the federation of all trade unions, and the Conference closed with a vote of thanks to the Rev. William Morris for placing the venue of our Conference, without charge, at our disposal.

* . * * * * *

I shall never forget as long as I live my first visit to Swansea. As soon as I arrived at the station I was met by a very old man of the name of Webber. He worked in the sulphur and ammonia departments of the Swansea Gas Works, and had come to extend the hospitality of his humble home to me. He asked me if I had arranged to stay at the hotel, and I told him that the money allowed me for travelling expenses was not sufficient to stay at a coffee-house, let alone an hotel. The old man then asked me to go with him to his cottage. It was adjacent to the Swansea Gas Works. It was about 8.30 on a winter's night when we arrived at his place. I found the floors were made of stone slabs ; there was hardly any furniture in the house, just a table and a few chairs, and the upstairs' rooms were simple and rugged. The old man provided me with food and tea, the best that he could afford, and made me comfortable. I contented myself with this simple and rough hospitality in what, I think, is the humblest cottage I have ever stayed in. I appreciated the kindness of these people, for I have never been, even in days of comparative affluence, a man to indulge in five-course meals or the luxury of the best hotels. I look back on that organising visit to Swansea as one of the happy human memories in my earlier days of struggle.

On my return to London from this visit I was given an assistant secretary to help me with my work. His name was William Ward, a big-hearted Irishman, who

had been working at the Greenwich Gas Works. He
enabled me to travel about much more than I had in
the past and to consolidate the many branches of the
union that had been, and were being, formed in different parts of the country.

One of my first trips, after being given the help of an
assistant secretary, was to Leeds, where I was concerned in the worst struggle in my career.

The Leeds Gas Committee, like other employers,
thought the time had arrived to take back from the gas
workers their new-won rights and concessions. They
demanded that the gas workers should engage themselves for a period of four months and forego their right
to strike within that period. They also wanted the
stokers to do twenty-five per cent. more work during
their eight-hour shift than they had been doing.

The situation was becoming serious. My Executive
Council was summoned to discuss the position. I took
the view that the dispute was one of great importance
to the future of the union, and I had no doubt but that
the men would strike if the corporation insisted on
pressing their demands. I also knew that they would
want financial assistance from the union.

After our long series of strikes there was little money
in the treasury, but the executive agreed with me and
voted the last £300 that we had in the bank.

When I arrived in Leeds I found that the Gas Committee had, in addition to the demands I have already
mentioned, decided to change the custom of discharging
in the slack season the last men to be taken on in the
busy season. They had given all the men in the retort
houses their notices.

Great excitement prevailed amongst the men. I
immediately called a mass meeting. Cunninghame
Graham was one of the speakers, and it was decided
that all the men should strike on the next day. The
Gas Committee had prepared for trouble. They had
organised men in different parts of the country to take
the places of the strikers as soon as they came out.

That Sunday evening I met Tom Mann. We were in the neighbourhood of the gas works at the time and could hear carpenters at work preparing sleeping accommodation for the blacklegs inside the works.

I said to Tom Mann : " You'll see some excitement to-morrow, Tom, if they attempt to bring blacklegs in here."

The plant was known as the Wortley Gas Works, and on the Sunday night, when the shifts came off, the strike began. We were prepared.

One of the local leaders, Tom Paylor, had heard that a number of blacklegs was to arrive at the New Wortley station at three o'clock in the morning. He chalked this information on the pavements in different parts of the city, and when the time arrived hundreds of strikers were in the vicinity.

The police were also in evidence in large numbers, but we had decided that no blackleg would go into the works without a fight, despite the great odds we were facing in challenging both the police and the blacklegs.

The police, hearing of our intention, diverted the blacklegs to the Town Hall, with a view to avoiding a conflict. This manœuvre did not succeed. We sent a mass picket to watch the Town Hall, but other lots of blacklegs were arriving.

One lot that was being escorted to the works was attacked by the crowd. Sticks and stones were used, and the police and the blacklegs were badly handled. When they arrived at the works the strikers and their hundreds of sympathisers made another charge. Most of the blacklegs got inside the works, but not without many casualties amongst them and the police. After the charge the pavements were strewn with hats, caps and policemen's helmets.

During that day the excitement was at a high pitch. Fights took place in different parts of the town. Early in the afternoon a sensation was caused when the Mayor posted notices in various parts of the town. This was considered equivalent to the reading of the Riot Act, and soldiers were being held in readiness for any eventuality.

By five o'clock in the afternoon enormous crowds had gathered in the streets, and by six o'clock the main thoroughfares were almost impassable. By seven o'clock the position everywhere was worse. The blacklegs were still heavily guarded within the Town Hall, and police and soldiers were all about the town.

Just before eight o'clock the storm broke. The blacklegs, guarded by the police, started their march from the Town Hall to the works. Every approach to the works was guarded by thousands of people. A railway bridge that crossed one of the streets alongside the works was thick with men and women. They were armed with stones and large sleepers of wood that they intended throwing at the blacklegs as they passed beneath.

The police and the soldiers realised the danger of the situation, but were unable to cope with it. When the procession reached this position, soldiers, policemen, and blacklegs came under a barrage of heavy missiles. They were completely at the mercy of the crowd, and many casualties took place amongst them.

After about twenty minutes the entrance to the gas yard was reached, when thousands of people, shouting and hooting, pushed towards the entrance. The soldiers made a guard near the gates, but as soon as they were opened and the blacklegs made to enter, the crowd rushed in. I was with them.

We charged at the blacklegs, who, in their terror, made a rush for a wall, over which many of them escaped. The police counter-attacked. I received a terrible blow on the back of the neck and went down like a bullock. When I recovered consciousness and looked around me, I found that many of my colleagues had also been badly hit.

The blacklegs had had enough. When they got inside the works, their main care was not to make gas, but to get out of the town as quickly as they possibly could ! We aided them in their escape, and thousands of people cheered them as they departed in various directions.

The ambulances, infirmaries, and hospitals were kept busy, and encounters continued to take place between strikers and their sympathisers on the one side and the police and the soldiers on the other.

I was approached by an inspector of the police, who threatened to arrest me if I did not clear out. I defied him, however, and declared my right to fight for the men. From then on, wherever I went, I was shadowed and watched by several policemen, and I was amongst a large number summoned for rioting.

The following day most of the blacklegs were provided with food and money and escorted to the railway station, where they left for their various homes.

The union paid the fares of many of them, and they were glad to get out of the town. Many that I spoke to swore that they would never be persuaded to take work again when a strike was on.

The Gas Committee soon found that they could not carry on the works, and after four days they gave way, paid off the few remaining blacklegs, and reinstated all the strikers.

All the summonses issued against myself and others were withdrawn as a result of public protest against the union-smashing efforts of the Gas Committee. Protests were made in the churches and chapels throughout the city, and public opinion was unanimous in condemning the employers for their methods on this occasion.

This was one of the greatest of victories both for the union and for the workers who so wholeheartedly supported the strikers. Shortly after I returned to London Frederick Engels sent me Karl Marx's

" Capital," in two volumes, in which he inscribed these words : " To Will Thorne, the victor of the Leeds battle, with fraternal greetings from Frederick Engels." This gift I prize very highly, both as a remembrance of the dispute and in memory of the great collaborator with Karl Marx that gave it to me.

CHAPTER VIII

A GREAT moment in my life was coming. Labour's parliament—the Trade Union Congress—was to be held at Liverpool, and I was to attend as a delegate representing my union. I was to make my first speech before this great body of workers' representatives.

It was a unique Congress in many ways. It was the largest that had then been held, representative for the first time not only of the skilled workers, but of the hitherto despised unskilled and general labourers. Peculiar trades were represented—gold beaters and match makers, book folders and dockers, chain makers, scissor grinders, and shirt and collar makers contributed to the discussions.

The leaders of the New Unionism were all present, many of them for the first time—Tom Mann, John Burns, Ben Tillett, myself, and several others. The advent of these representatives, with a strong voting power at Congress, led to many exciting rows. During one debate John Burns was given a very poor hearing by the old school of trade unionists. John mounted the table and, amidst howling and cat calls, defied the old school, and finally delivered his speech on the question of the legal eight-hour day.

Another stir was caused when James MacDonald, secretary of the Tailors' Union, told Congress that the clothes of the Prince of Wales were made in a room where a case of small-pox had been found.

Discussions were very lively. Jimmy MacDonald moved that no parliamentary candidate should receive the support of working men unless he declared himself in favour of nationalistion of land, shipping, railways, and other means of production and distribution. John Burns, after saying that he would simply second the motion, showed his sense of humour by proceeding to deliver a lengthy speech. Throughout the Congress the New Unionists forced the pace. We were successful in getting the Parliamentary Committee of the Congress to agree to send representatives to the forthcoming International Congress that was to be held in Brussels the following year. Finally my great moment arrived. It was on the eight-hour question. Many delegates had had their say before I could catch the chairman's eye. At last my turn came. I was somewhat nervous at making my maiden speech. My thoughts rushed through my head in a wild turmoil. I had prepared no notes, but my intimate knowledge and the disputes I had gone through on the eight-hour question made me feel very deeply about the matter.

With the force of passion behind my tongue, I jumped right into my argument by saying that there were only two ways of getting an eight-hour working day—one by striking, and the other by Act of Parliament.

A great burst of cheering followed this first remark of mine. Confidence came to me at once. My nervousness disappeared, and I proceeded to tell the delegates how my union to the extent of 30,000—half the membership—had been able to secure the eight-hour day, and how they had also found the employers spending as much as £100,000 in an attempt to break my union ; not only that, but giving the police bribes amounting to £600 for the purpose of kicking and cuffing my members in different parts of London. I appealed with all the powers at my command to the delegates to support me to obtain a universal eight-hour day. After elaborating my appeal, I sat down, half in a dream and terribly excited, amidst a wonderful and heartening burst of applause and cheering. I have made many speeches at Trade Union Congresses since that time, but none do I remember so vividly or which affected me more than that maiden speech.

Finally the resolution of the New Unionists on the eight-hour question was carried by a majority of thirty-eight, and we were wild with enthusiasm.

The exciting and passionate scenes that took place at this Congress made a Roman holiday for the " penny-a-line " journalists; it was, however, not the new revolutionary delegates that were abusive and ill-mannered, but the champions of the old reactionary school, who, whenever one of us rose to speak, yelled at us, shouted, stamped their feet, blew railway whistles, and generally created pandemonium, refusing to listen to us, and preventing others from doing so that wanted to. It is, I think, true, as Cunninghame Graham said, " vanity, egoism, and self-advertisement " had something to do with the disorder; perhaps one or two of the New Unionists were a little blatant and a little too anxious when they spoke that no other dog should bark, but we set an admirable example of good-humoured patience under much unfairness and provocation. Looking over the reports of the Congress, I find that the New Unionists rarely interrupted; they spoke little and respected the chair. Once or twice they had to protest. Stung by the boorishness of the old school, I jumped to my feet and hurled this rebuke at them, when they jeered and laughed at one of the general labour representatives: " A firewood cutter is as good as an engineer. Are you only going to listen to engineers, and not to unskilled workers ? " I was wild with rage, but my reprimand went home, and the speaker that I had interceded for was from then onwards given a fairer hearing. Many of the scenes that marked the Conference were due to trade, personal differences, and jealousies between the crafts. The rising of a joiner to speak was like a red rag to a bull on the shipwrights, and the war between these two closely allied trades was furious and bitter, especially when Mr. Gould, a joiner from Hull, tried to speak.

Clashes often took place between the two miners' groups—Durham and Northumberland being one section, and all the other mining areas the other. It was, however, one of these little clashes that was responsible for the finest moment of a very interesting week. Cowey, a miners' delegate, rose, full of splendid power and wonderful eloquence, calling on God to wither his hand, that he held high in the air, if he had any wish or desire but that of helping his fellow-men. That was the first Trade Union Congress that I attended. I have been present at every one that has been held since, but never has there been such animated discussion, and I believe that the expression of feeling that took place has in the end been the means of securing greater solidarity and brotherhood in the Trade Union Movement.

Returning to London tired but happy, I had anticipated having a short holiday. I had been working hard practically day and night for nearly two years. Not alone was the work arduous, but I carried a great responsibility. I did not complain, as my wife, who suffered, perhaps, more than I did, never grumbled. Her help and interest in my work gave me great satisfaction and solace. But there was to be no holiday for me.

On returning to London I found that some evilly disposed person, or persons, through the columns of an unfriendly Press, were endeavouring to create an eruption between the Gas Light and Coke Company and their employees. Report had been spread that it was the intention of the men to go on strike in the winter season.

The company, believing these reports, made application to the War Office to supply them with some thousands of labourers. The Government also promised to provide soldiers, supplied with twenty rounds of ball cartridge per man, for the purpose of maintaining order. Applications were also made to the Home Secretary for police and other assistance.

The reports that had been circulated stated that the men at the Beckton Gas Works, the largest in the world, would refuse to work with non-unionists, and that an immediate lightning strike was contemplated. The Home Secretary communicated with the War Office, and a joint meeting of the civil and military authorities was held, at which it was decided to draft, if necessary, troops into the extensive works at Beckton.

We had, however, never discussed the question of a strike, nor had we any intention of calling one. The company, nevertheless, did not believe us, and temporary buildings were erected inside the works for the purpose of feeding and housing blacklegs in the event of a strike or a lock-out.

The commander of the garrison at Chatham was notified to hold troops in readiness for special duty. These troops were Royal Marines and Royal Engineers. They were paraded in the morning and served with twenty rounds of ball cartridge each, but they were kept in ignorance of their destination and their possible duty.

Government tugs were standing by with steam up, ready to leave at a moment's notice for the Beckton Gas Works, which fronts the river. The men were paraded at midday, but, as no orders had arrived from headquarters, they were dismissed to barracks. Again in the evening they were paraded, but following my efforts to get a conference with the company, instructions were sent cancelling the orders for the troops to stand by for their special duties. At the conference that I had with the employers I told them definitely that the union had no intention whatsoever of calling a strike at the works. It was true that we wanted only the employment of union men, but if the company would not agree to this suggestion, we were not pressing the question to the extent of a dispute. After a little further discussion, we calmed the fears of the company, and amicable relations were resumed.

With due modesty, I claim that my Executive Com-

mittee and myself averted what would have been a
most disastrous calamity by the action we took on this
matter. It was obviously a plot of some one to smash
the union, or to bring it into disrepute. I have no
doubt that great loss of life would have taken place if
I, with my colleagues, had been unable to get the
company to act as reasonably as they did in a very
tense situation. I am sure that, if a crisis had been
precipitated, it would not have meant only a strike or
a lock-out at the gas works, but, such was the temper of
all workers at that time, that a general strike would
have taken place that would have inevitably led to
civil war. The straightening out of this tangle was my
holiday.

Immediately on my return to London I started out
on an organising tour in the West of England and did
not get back again to London until the day before
Christmas.

Up to this time I had never spent a peaceful Christmas, and I was looking forward to a few days' rest and
comfort in my own home.

A letter was waiting for me from Dr. Aveling. He
told me in his letter that Paul Lefargue was spending
the Christmas holidays with him and was anxious to
see and know something of the poverty and the slums
in the East End of London.

My home was close to the Canning Town Station and
I asked them both to come along and see me. We spent
a happy and fraternal hour or two on Christmas Eve
until 10.30 in the evening. Then I took them out to
show them some of the sights of the East End.

We started in the Tidal Basin area, in Jack Jones'
Parliamentary Division. But we had not gone far
when we met a group of " coalies." They were members
of my union, and had just finished the dirty work of
unloading a coal boat. The coal they had been handling
was known as " Navigation Steam," the dustiest of all
coals, and the men were as black as niggers from the
dust. One of the men was carrying a big two-gallon

bottle on his shoulder tied with a piece of rope. Paul Lefargue asked Dr. Aveling, in broken English, what this bottle was for, and I explained that it was used for carrying beer which the men took to work with them because the men could not keep drinking tea or cocoa, or even water. Paul Lefargue was highly interested in this, and said that he had never seen such a thing before.

From Tidal Basin we went along to Custom House, which is close to the Victoria Docks. Here the crowded streets had the atmosphere of a sordid carnival. The public-houses were emptying their customers into the street : some were gay and singing, others maudlin and weeping. Arguments and disputes were taking place in the different little knots of people. We ran into an awful row that was taking place between some sailors and a crowd of crimps and crooks, that used to frequent the haunts of sailor men with the object of robbing them when they were paid off.

Often when a sailor got into the clutches of these people he would wake up to find himself stripped of the new clothes that it is his habit to buy on his return home from a voyage, and in their place to be wearing a brown paper suit or old and discarded garments, and not a penny of his hard earned money in his pocket.

The sharks were evidently unlucky in picking their victims on this occasion. One of the sailors was a broad-chested big Norwegian who knew how to use his fists. He had already knocked out two of the sharks, and his companions were giving him able assistance. Reinforcements were coming to the assistance of the harrassed crooks. No police were in sight and the row was getting worse when I said, " Let us get out of this or we will be dragged into the thick of it."

We walked along Connaught Road. Near the station is the main entrance to the Albert Docks, and I showed them one of the familiar sights of this place at night time, a crowd of women who are always waiting to meet the sailors and firemen that work on the ships. We

turned from this towards the famous Ratcliffe Highway, a sordid street that has been made famous, and
which is known all over the world by frequent references
to it in sailor men's chanties. The highway was about
a mile and a half from where we were at the time, and
as we were crossing the Iron Bridge that divides Poplar
from Canning Town we met Tom Walsh, an organiser
of the Sailors' and Firemen's Union. He had been in
the big 1889 dock strike. I introduced him to Paul
Lefargue ; he knew Dr. Aveling. I told him what we
were doing, and he volunteered to take us to Ratcliffe
Highway and show us some of the sights, and to reveal
some of the mysteries of Chinatown.

Some of the lodging-houses were weird, dark and
uncanny places, pervaded with a strange, exotic smell.
The passages in them were very narrow, and Chinamen with bowed heads and slippered feet moved
stealthily about.

After warning us to be silent and to follow him, Tom
took us to a doorway that had strange red slips of
paper with Chinese characters on it plastered all over
the door. He opened the door and, following him we
saw a counter, behind which sat a wizened old Chinaman, the shelves behind him filled with different kinds
of Oriental merchandise. Tom leaned over and spoke
to him, but we did not hear what he said. It must
have been satisfactory, however, for the Chinaman
came out from behind the counter, shut the door by
which we had entered and slid a big bolt into position. Then he took us down a long, unlighted passage.
At the end of this passage we came to a room in which
stood a gilt Chinese idol, or " joss " as they call it.
Glasses, in which were burning sticks of incense, were
around the base of the joss, and comfortable cushions,
of rich quality and colour, lay about the room amongst
the other Oriental fittings and furnishings.

Again there was a whispered consultation between
Tom and the Chinaman, after which we were led into
another room. In this room a long, low platform, about

eighteen inches high and about six foot wide, ran the whole length of the wall. It was covered with matting. On it were lying at one end two Chinamen who had between them a little peanut oil lamp and a thick-stemmed opium pipe. At the other end was a well-dressed and apparently respectable woman. Opposite her was a Chinaman who, with a hairpin-like needle, was taking some of the sticky black opium out of a little receptacle which he twirled over the peanut oil lamp, making it into a pill. The pill cooked, he placed it in the centre of the bowl of the pipe, which looked like a door-knob. He then pierced it with one end of the needle and gave the pipe to the woman. She placed the pill right over the flame and took one long inhalation of the smoke. This, it was explained to us, was the way opium is smoked. We were told that people from all stratas of society were addicted to the habit of opium smoking, and that it was an expensive pleasure, or vice, whichever you prefer to call it.

By this time both Dr. Aveling and Paul Lefargue had seen enough of the sights of the East End for one night, so we started for home again. Near the East India Dock gates we met that wonderful old man, beloved of the East End people, Will Crooks. He was just coming from a meeting. I introduced him to my two friends, and then we went on to my home where we finished Christmas Eve.

On Christmas morning I showed them round the old Canning Town slum area, which is in my own Parliamentary Division—an area that is worse even than Tidal Basin, Custom House, or Silvertown.

Paul Lefargue asked me, through Dr. Aveling, whether there were any Labour men on the Town Council. I told him that there were not, but that there were one or two Liberals and Radicals. I told him that it was my object to get the Canning Town slums torn down from end to end, and to have the whole place rebuilt with proper sanitary dwelling houses. I told him that I was prospective candidate in the forthcoming elections for

the Town Council. Paul Lefargue thanked me for his
interesting experience, and said that he would always
remember his Christmas visit to my house at Canning
Town and what I had told him.

The beginning of the year 1891 found the union in a
very weak financial position ; we had gone through an
extraordinary number of strikes and lock-outs, and
the drain on our resources had left us with only
£227 4s. to bring forward. The employers could not
understand how we were able to pay out of the small
contribution of 2d. per week per member the amount
of dispute pay that we did. This was due to the fact
that we only paid strike and lock-out pay. We had
so many different sections of workers in the union—it
was a federation in itself—that while money was paid
out to men in dispute, contributions were coming in
from thousands of other workers in other trades and
industries. I am certain that this was the cause of the
real success of the union, and I firmly believe that if this
principle was carried out on a larger scale by all workers,
in this and other countries, it would prevent the
employers from imposing upon them the conditions
that they do.

Early in the new year employers all over the country
were beginning to take advantage of the workers.
They had seen the success of Mr. George Livesey's
attack on the London gas workers, and they had
decided to check the workers in their demands for
increased wages and shorter hours that were being
made in different parts of the country. They were, in
fact, following the example of the workers by organising
their forces. When the new Trade Union Movement
started we only had to fight individual concerns, but
now the employers were beginning to form themselves
into federations and combines, and the trade unions
were finding their tasks of protecting and increasing
wages and conditions much more difficult.

There were about twenty-five different strikes going
on at the time, the most important was the strike in

Dublin of coal porters and canal workers. The coal porters were asking for 25 per cent. increase in wages and alterations in their method of working ; the canal workers were striking for a 15 per cent. increase in their wages—this they gained after being on strike only two days.

The coal porters were a different proposition ; there were about 250 of them on strike and they cost us a lot of money in strike pay. I must say that the Dublin coal porters were about the worst set of men I have ever had to deal with. Their work was the loading and unloading of coal vessels.

When the strike started I was sent by my Executive Council, with a man by the name of Mike Cantry, to Dublin to pay the men the strike pay. It took us three nights to do it. On the first night we could only pay about fifty of them, because they were so noisy and high spirited, and also because it took us some time to examine their cards, to see whether they were in compliance with the union rules. I found that a good number of the men were very much in arrears, and that some of them had not been in the union six months and were, therefore, not entitled to benefit. The ones that were not entitled to benefit I told to stand aside and come along the following evening. The second night the trouble was worse, because the men who were entitled to be paid were taking sides with the men who were not. We paid about 150 men on the second night, and on the third night, after we had finished the balance of the men, matters got very exciting. An animated and passionate discussion, or I should say, argument, between myself and the men who were not entitled to pay took place ; they were abusive, and threatened to throw me and my assistant through the window. I could defend myself against any one single handed, but fifty big strong Irish coal porters was more than I and my companion were prepared to tackle. In a flash I made up my mind. I whispered to Mike, and we made a dash for the door and down some stone steps leading from a dilapidated building. The men followed us excited and angry; they tried to get our money bag, but we managed to get to the bottom of the stairs and did a flying sprint for the hotel where we were staying, somewhere in Sackville Street. We arrived there safely, but it was the fastest and one of the most exciting moments in my life as a trade union official. The union was very strong in Ireland, having over 20,000 members, and when we came to settle the strike we found that the employers were very annoyed because the Irish coal porters and other workers were so effectively organised with the English workers. They wanted to know what right the English trade unions had to interfere with the Irish workers, and what they could do for them that they could not do for themselves. These employers were some of the roughest type of men I have ever had to deal with, but, despite this, we secured for the men all that they were striking for.

The coal porters in London were also well organised in our union; we had a large number of them working at the Victoria Docks, where the dockers and the sailors and firemen were in dispute with the new powerful Shipping Federation. The steamship *Shagbrook* came to the dock to be bunkered with coal, and the secretary of my coal porters' branch came to me to know what should be done about the matter. I at once gave instructions that the men should refuse to coal the ship, and it left the dock with its bunkers practically empty.

Across the river on the south side a strike had started at a big tannery works at Deptford and Bermondsey. These men were not organised in the big trade union of that area known as the South Side Labour Protection League. This organisation would not accept these workers, so we took them into our union, and later on organised all sorts of other workers in different factories and workshops in this district.

As well as strikes and lock-outs, we had our legal battles. One of these cropped up over the custom of the employers in the brickfields holding back so many pence on each thousand of bricks made until the end of the season. It often happened that men were dismissed from work and did not get their " back pence." We made a test case of one of these occurrences and took it to the courts ; we won the case, and since that time the system of " back pence " has entirely disappeared.

Frequent calls were made upon us by other unions, to which we always responded if it was at all possible. In this way we gave £150 to the men on strike on the Scottish Railways, and sent £300 to the Australian workers, who were also involved in a big dispute with their employers. This was a practical way of expressing our gratitude for the assistance they had given the British workers in the 1889 dock strike.

Tragedy and sorrow came into my life with a chilling suddenness. My wife was taken ill suddenly, and died in a few days.

The cause of her death was a fever brought about through defective drains that passed beneath the house. It is such tragedies as this that make us dwellers of the slums a little bitter at times in our fight to secure more habitable and hygienic homes.

My wife took ill on a Friday night. It was a sad week end, for as I looked at her I realised that only a miracle would save her life. Dr. Moira, a labour colleague of mine, used all his skill and knowledge to try and save her, but she died on the Monday morning.

After my wife died I became father and mother to six children, three boys and three girls. It was almost an impossible task, and my sister Clara, who was then living in Birmingham, came down to London and kept house for me.

My elder son, Will, was full of mischief and took a lot of handling. One day, when he had been particularly cheeky, I gave him a licking. He got up and went out of the house, slamming the door behind him, and shouting through the key hole : " I'm not coming home to-night."

I at once got up and went out after him. He was
making all haste down the street, but I finally caught
him and brought him home again, where I made him
sit down and write a statement, promising that he
would never do such a thing again.

My wife had only been dead nine months when the
dark hand of death again reached into my home and
claimed my baby boy, who was only about a year
old.

Will did not lose his mischievousness as he grew up.
One day, when he was working on a foreign timber
barge, at a wharf in Old Canning Town, he sailed away
with it, and for over a week we heard nothing of him,
until late one evening he returned home again.

When we asked him where he had been, he told us :
" Only for a bit of a sail."

I felt like giving him a bit of a strap, but instead I
gave him a bit of my tongue. It made no impression
on him however.

After he married he joined the Territorials and,
although he had been a high-spirited lad in his single
days, he was a very good husband and father. On the
outbreak of war he joined one of the Essex regiments.
When he was home on leave from the front he showed
us a watch, postcards and several souvenirs he had
taken from a German. I learnt that his regiment
was in a particular part of the line, where every night a
number of men were being sniped, but no one knew
from where the shots came. One night my boy crept
out into No Man's Land and discovered a German
sniper up a tree. My son shot him and so obtained the
souvenirs.

I have seen him do just as brave things at home.
One night when I was with him we passed a crowd of
bookmakers and roughs in trouble with the police.
One of them had whipped out a knife, with the intention of using it on a policeman. My son saw this and
made a dash for the man, making him drop the knife.
He did a similar thing on another occasion, for which

he was complimented by the Chief of Police and given a reward for his pluck.

I lost this lad at Ypres in one of the battles of 1917.

Being a widower I found was a lonely life, although I had my sister and the five children at home. My thoughts again turned to matrimony.

My office was at the top of Mr. Byford's house, and his daughter, Emily, would come into my office quite often to light the fire and tidy up the place. We would have long talks together, and I remember her lovely head of hair which hung down below her waist. I found myself becoming very fond of her and I felt that my fondness for her was being reciprocated, so I asked her father if he would like me for a son-in-law.

Mr. Byford said he had no objection, but, because of the age of his daughter—she was only twenty-three— he thought it would be rather a handful for her to look after my five children. I told him that I realised that, and after I had promised to make her life as easy as possible he gave his consent.

It was a bright sunny morning in the early summer. I had just returned from the provinces, where I had been doing some organising work. As I entered my office, Emily was silhouetted against the window, the sun was streaming through her hair and all about her. She had just finished tidying the room.

It was a neat and beautiful picture. My loneliness and the love that had been growing in my heart surged up within me. I asked her to marry me, and half-sobbing in my arms she stammered her acceptance.

We were married at the Holy Trinity Church in Barking Road. She was twenty-three, I was thirty-seven. At our wedding breakfast lots of friends were present, including Dr. Aveling and Eleanor Marx-Aveling. We spent our honeymoon at the little town of Seaford, where our married life nearly came to an abrupt end.

This happened when we went for a sail one morning. We had got a little way off from the shore when a squall came up and our little boat was tossed about and threatened with swamping every minute. Finally, as we got near the shore, a big wave caught us and did swamp the boat.

We had a terrific struggle to get ashore and there was great excitement amongst the crowd of people watching us. We were soaked to the skin and looked, and felt, half-drowned ! We went straight home and changed our clothes. I thought this was rather a good start for a honeymoon ! There were six children by my second marriage, and they get on exceedingly well with the children of my first wife.

The Avelings and my family were very great friends, and when they moved to Orpington in Kent at about this time we still visited them. Eleanor was very fond of children and my eldest daughter often went to stay with her. She was also passionately fond of her husband, Dr. Aveling, and very devoted to him. Her death was a real dramatic tragedy. She committed suicide because of the infidelity of her husband. Dr. Aveling was a dramatic critic and wrote for several of the newspapers. Sometimes he helped to produce amateur theatricals. One of the plays, in which Mr. H. W. Lee also played, was called " The Railway Guard." In this play was a woman with whom Dr. Aveling became very familiar. The news broke Eleanor's heart when she heard of it. She was a brave woman to the last ; her heart broken with the news and her mind overwrought with the realisation of what it meant, she went home, stripped herself of her day clothes, and, dressed in white, laid herself out on a bed and took prussic acid. Dr. Aveling did not live long after this. He was ostracised by his many friends and colleagues for the way he had treated his wife, and he finally committed suicide in a flat at Battersea about three years after the death of his wife.

Before he died he asked me if there was anything belonging to Eleanor that I would like. He knew the great admiration that I had for her, and the friendship that existed between us. He told me to go to the house and take what I wanted, and I still have a rocking-chair and a copper kettle of hers that I keep in her memory. But for this tragedy I believe that Eleanor would have still been living, and would have been a greater woman's leader than the greatest of contemporary women.

The Avelings were both very earnest Internationalists. From them I learnt much about the necessity for co-operation between the workers of the different countries ; through them I met most of the leading thinkers and advocates of the working classes in the different European countries. I remember them taking me to meet Fred Engels at his house in Regent's Park. It was on Engels' seventieth birthday. At this meeting with Engels there was also present Paul Lefargue, Mr. and Mrs. Bernstein, Herr Liebknecht and Herr Bebel. It was a most interesting gathering. During the evening Fred Engels told us some very interesting incidents about what happened during his life-time. I believe he made his money in the textile industries in Lancashire. He also told us some very interesting things about his experiences in the international and national movement. He had a good deal to say about Russia, as he had just written some interesting articles on the foreign policy of Russian Czardom. I think he started from 1774 and traced the history of Russia right up to that date ; not only Russia, but Greece, Austria, Spain, Italy, Turkey and Poland. He was a vigorous old man, even at that time, and spoke for three-quarters of an hour. I don't think any one in this or any other country at the time could teach him anything about the revolutionary move-ment in any country. Herr Liebknecht told us of his long history with the Socialist and Labour Movement in Germany, and about the number of years he had been in prison through taking an active part in the Labour and Socialist Movement. Bebel and Zinger told us many in-teresting things, while the Avelings and myself reviewed the rapid growth of the trade union movement since our union started in 1889. Our foreign comrades were astonished to learn how the movement had grown in the short period of its existence, and they asked me whether there would be any stability about it or whether in the course of twelve or eighteen months the whole movement would fall away. I told them that so far as I was concerned I thought the movement had come to stay, because of the way in which the employers had been dealing with the wage earners in all parts of the country, and I stated I would be very much surprised if at any time the movement fell away. I said, " We may have the ups and downs in the times of depression and good trade." I told them that the time had come to bring about closer organised relations between the Labour parties of the different countries. The most immediate question, I declared, was that of preventing the introduction from one country to another of unfair labour, *i.e.*, of workers, who, not knowing the conditions of the labour struggle in a particular country, are imported into that country by the capitalists in order to reduce the wages and lengthen the hours of labour, or both. The most practical way to carry this out appeared to me by appointing in each country a secretary who would communicate with a secretary in the different countries, and the moment any dispute arose between labour and capital in any one country it would be known by all the others, who would make it their business to prevent the sending of labour to the country affected. I asked them to get the unions in their different countries to agree to this system of communication and assistance, and I promised to get my union to do this as far as England was concerned. From that day to this my union has always been closely associated with the International Trade and Labour Movement.

It was a very pleasant gathering. We had very nice food and some excellent wine, that was served by Mrs. Kautsky, Mr. Engels' housekeeper. Mr. Engels presented me on this occasion with several books, and

from time to time sent me different volumes dealing
with economics and the philosophy of Socialism.

At the next conference of the union we decided to
send delegates to the International Conference to be
held in Brussels. I was appointed a delegate, and made
my first trip to the Continent on this occasion. The
Conference lasted almost a week and was held at the
Maison du Peuple.

William Morris, Keir Hardie, Harry Quelch, and many
foreign delegates were present. The Maison du Peuple
was a very large building. The headquarters of the
Belgian trade unionists, it was also a centre for social
gatherings, and during the week we had the pleasure of
attending some splendid concerts. I was struck by
the amount of light lager beer that was drunk. It was
very nice too.

One evening before we left Brussels a party of us
visited a *café*. Outside this *café* there was a notice,
but as it was in French I could not read it, so I asked
one of the party to translate it for me, but I was told to
wait until after we came out. We had a very enjoyable
meal and when we came out of the *café* I again asked
that the notice be translated, and this is what it meant :
" Only horseflesh served at this *café*." For a moment
or two I was a little upset, but as I had enjoyed the
meal I quickly got over the idea of having eaten horseflesh.

My next International Congress took me to Zurich.
George Bernard Shaw attended this Congress. Writing
to me the other day he reminded me of it and what
happened there. He says in his letter :—

" You were then a remarkably fine young man ;
and I was not yet old enough to be your father,
though I am now. I was with Sydney [now Lord]
Olivier. The weather was very hot, and when the
Congress adjourned for lunch every day we were all
sweltering. You always made a dash for the lake ;
and Olivier and I did the same. You seemed to be

extraordinarily strong physically : for you swam like
a centaur, breast high out of the water, to the admiration of all spectators and the envy of all the sculptors,
though you were quite unconscious of attracting any
notice, and just revelled in the coolness of the lake."

Bernard Shaw also remarks that the experience at
Zurich left him with very friendly impressions of
myself, and that when my name began to appear in the
papers, as I went from success to success in the Labour
Movement, the news always meant something to him
when most of the other names meant nothing.

I witnessed one of the most extraordinary demonstrations that I have ever seen the Sunday that we
were in Zurich. Thousands of young children, in snow-
white dresses with bright red sashes across their
shoulders, marched with men and women through the
town. The procession was led by excellent brass bands,
and the line was made gay with gaily coloured banners
on which were inscribed various mottoes.

During my stay in Zurich I visited several of the
public-houses ; they are quite different to ours in
England. My object was to get first-hand information
from the people that used them. I learnt that compulsory military service was the law of the country, but
I was surprised to learn that during such service the
people kept their own rifles at home.

Passing through the streets I saw another strange
thing : the use of dogs as beasts of burden. Large
dogs were harnessed to small carts, and went about
their work just as horses and ponies do in this country.
I saw a man pulling a cart up a hill and a big dog went
behind pushing the cart and so helping his master.
Turning to my companion I said, " It appears to me
the bosses would make a monkey work if it would be
cheaper than dogs or men."

At the Congress the Anti-Parliamentary Commune
Anarchists were in full force. During the week there
was quite a breeze caused by them, Fighting com-

menced and knives were used ; happily there were no serious casualties.

London was the venue of the next International, and a demonstration was organised in Hyde Park on the Sunday after the Congress opened. It turned out a very wet day. I was with my wife, and we, like every one else, got soaking wet, and the paint was nearly all washed out of the banners that were carried in the procession.

One afternoon during the Congress a big Italian delegate, who had been creating a certain amount of trouble, took a seat on the platform. I was asked to remove him, but not being able to speak Italian, and as he did not understand English, I could not tell him that he had to get off the platform. As I endeavoured to make him understand what I meant, he became hostile, and when I tried to get hold of him he pulled out a knife about nine inches long ! Thinking discretion the better part of valour, I retreated, and finally one of the translators cooled the Italian down and persuaded him to leave the platform.

I only spent a few days in Paris, where the next International was held, as the dissolution of the British Parliament had taken place, and I had been asked by the workers of West Ham to take part in the fight, so I had to leave Paris and return to West Ham to get the political organisation in working order for the election.

I met the great Jean Jaurés, whom France has just honoured by placing his remains with other national heroes in the Pantheon, at my next International Conference, held at Amsterdam. Harry Quelch, Hyndman, Bebel and Mrs. Bridges Adams were present at this Congress, which was marked by many stormy and animated debates. During one of the debates Jaurés attacked the German leaders for their adoption of Parliamentary tactics. This caused a storm, and another row broke out on the debate upon the question of what attitude the working class should adopt in future wars. It was during this debate that Bebel declared, " There will be one more European war, but it will be the last." This Congress was held just at the conclusion of the Russo-Japanese War, and at the end of the Congress a delegate from Japan and one from Russia stood on the platform and shook hands in a most friendly way. It was a dramatic little episode, more eloquent of fraternity than many speeches. The delegates cheered and cheered, for it had gone home to them that while the two countries had been at war there was no real animosity or hatred between the workers of these two countries.

At Stuttgart, Germany, a few years later I attended another International Conference. With wide streets and many open spaces, beautiful buildings, and many points of interest, I found Stuttgart a very pleasant place ; but what struck me more than anything else was the number of soldiers that were continually passing the hotel, and were even stationed outside the entrance.

I was told that the object of marching the soldiers past the hotels where the delegates were staying was to demonstrate the military power of Germany ! The display certainly had an effect on the delegates. Harry Quelch likened the Kaiser and his associates to the characters of the thieves' kitchen. This came to the ears of the Kaiser, who ordered Quelch to be out of the country within twelve hours, and he was unable to stay for the remainder of the Congress. During our stay in Stuttgart we were entertained in the big *Garten* near the town. The place was beautifully illuminated, and there was an abundance of food and wine. We had a merry time, but my memory fails me as to the details.

I only attended one more International before the outbreak of war—that was at Copenhagen. I found it a very clean place, and was struck by the odd, but very neat, clothing the people wore. During my stay in Copenhagen I moved about a lot amongst the people, and learnt much of their conditions and customs.

With the Right Hon. C. W. Bowerman, I was

appointed to attend the International Committee held in Paris in the middle of 1918. Just before leaving, their Royal Highnesses the Prince of Wales and Princess Mary had arranged to pay a visit to the London County Council offices to see a tablet that was being sent by the Labour Movement to America. Bowerman and I had also to attend this function. I had a long conversation with the Prince of Wales and with Princess Mary. Mr. Bowerman and I managed to get away from the County Hall at midday, which gave us very little time to get to Folkestone, where we were to catch the boat to Boulogne. Time was short, but the War Office placed one of their fastest motor cars at our disposal. Although the car travelled at a speed of over sixty miles an hour, we found that, when we got to Folkestone, we had missed the boat, and had to wait for the next one. Going across we had to wear lifebelts, for the submarine war was still on, and our boat was convoyed by torpedo-boat destroyers, that sailed along and circled about us. We arrived in Paris early in the evening. While we were in the hotel the warning gun was fired over the city that told us the German air raiders were " coming over." We were commanded to remain in the hotel. The raid lasted about an hour, and I could hear the bombs dropping and the explosion of the anti-aircraft shells. The German bombers did not, however, get past the outer defences.

I got to the railway station before my colleagues and got into the carriage that had been reserved for us. Inside the carriage, I put my umbrella through the handle of the door. A French colonel came along and tried to open the door ; finding the handle tight, he gave a hard push that broke my umbrella. When he got into the carriage, he started talking to me in the most excited manner. As I did not understand French, I did not know what he was talking about. Sydney Webb then arrived on the scene, and I explained to him what had happened and asked him to tender my apologies to the Frenchman.

Since Paris I have attended successive congresses at Geneva, the World's Peace Congress at the Hague, and at Amsterdam. I was present at the London Conference with Miss Bondfield, Jack Jones, the Right Hon. J. R. Clynes, and Ramsay MacDonald. I also made a trip to Rome to attend a Trade Union Congress International at which the Right Hon. J. H. Thomas was the chairman, and last year I was a British delegate to the International Trade Union Congress held in Vienna.

All these trips abroad have been very interesting ; the congresses and the interchange of ideas that has taken place has done much to bring about a greater understanding and feeling of brotherhood between all the workers in the different countries. There have been no spectacular developments, but I am sure that the foundation stones have been laid at these meetings for congresses of future peace among the nations, and complete unity and solidarity of the working class.

While I always laid great stress on the importance and necessity of these international gatherings, I have taken an even greater interest in the British Trade Union Congresses, where we have had to hammer out solutions to our own trade union and national problems. I have attended every Congress since 1889. I remember the Congress at Newcastle, where I met for the first time Mr. Thomas Burt, a great leader of the Northumberland miners. He was the president of the Congress, and made a very extraordinary speech without recourse to notes. During his presidential address Mr. Burt mentioned the struggle the engineers were engaged in at that time in trying to secure a nine-hour day in Newcastle and the surrounding districts. I must quote his remarks when referring to this topic, and to the fact that both the skilled and unskilled workers were represented : " All honour to the gas workers and general labourers and their general secretary, Mr. Will Thorne, who has so successfully organised these great masses," he said. When I heard these words, I felt like turning a somersault with joy, for, with all due modesty, I can say I was more than delighted with such recognition from a man like Burt, who was the leader of a long and well-organised body of skilled workers.

It was at this Congress that I was taken to task by the representatives of the skilled workers' union for taking into my union all kinds of general labourers, and because the contribution was only 2d. per week.

I told the delegates it was my intention to organise all kinds of general labourers, from the gravedigger to the parson. I said gravediggers are as much entitled to be organised as any other section of workers, for when they are working they do not know who is to be buried in the grave they are digging; it may be a member of the High or Low Church, it may be a duke, or it may be a dustman; death makes no distinction with men, and my union makes no distinction amongst general workers. As I proceeded with my speech, I am told that I almost became poetic till I returned again to the topic of organisation and told the delegates that it was also my intention to organise the badly-paid tripe dressers and sausage makers.

It was at this Congress that Keir Hardie called a number of the delegates together, including myself, to discuss the formation of the Independent Labour Party.

At the opening of the next Congress, held in Glasgow, the first news we received was that Keir Hardie and John Burns had just been elected Members of Parliament for the first time. It was at this Congress that my dear old friend Ben Tillett was elected to the Parliamentary Committee.

We had an exciting time at the next Congress that was held in Belfast. During Congress week the House of Lords threw out Gladstone's Home Rule Bill, and on the night of the defeat of the Bill in the House of Commons great excitement prevailed throughout the city. Bonfires and tar barrels were burnt in different parts of the city, and an effigy of Gladstone was carried through the streets and finally thrown on to one of

the bonfires.   Thousands of people of all religious
denominations gathered in their respective quarters of
the town, feeling ran high, and large numbers of
mounted and foot police were drafted into these areas
to prevent riots between Catholics and Protestants.
The delegates to Congress were warned not to express
themselves on the question of Home Rule, and many
of us were watched and guarded by detectives.   The
excitement lasted until early morning, and there were
rumblings and spasmodic demonstrations all during the
week.

During the week a big demonstration was held in one
of the parks.   Before the demonstration started I went
to the park and sat down on one of the seats.   I had
around my shoulders a big sash in the union colours
of red, white and green.   While I was sitting there a
man came up to me and said, " Governor, if you want
to keep your head intact, you'd better take that sash
off."   I said, " Why ? "   He said, " There's too much
green in it."   " Well, what about it ? " I said.   He
answered, " Don't you know that the Gladstone Home
Rule Bill has been thrown out of the House of Lords ? "
I said, " Yes."   " Well," he said, " people in this part
are not Home Rulers, and as green represents Home
Rule, you'd better take it off."   I heeded the man's
advice and took the sash off, but I told him that I felt
like defying them all.

In a little while the people began to gather around
the platform from which the speakers, including John
Burns and Ben Tillett, were to make their speeches.
The meeting had only started a few minutes, when in
the distance I saw a big procession of people marching
in military fashion towards us.   I turned to Burns,
who was standing alongside of me, and asked, " Who
are these fellows coming along, are they some of the
delegates ? "   He said, " I don't know, but it looks like
it."

The people round the platform made way for the
procession to come through, as they thought they were

some of the delegates, but, to the surprise of everybody, they turned to be a hostile crowd, and they prevented speeches being made. We got away as quickly as we could, for more serious trouble was threatening.

I caused quite a scene at Congress when I protested against the weakness of a resolution that was passed sympathising with the friends and relatives of three workmen who had been shot and killed by soldiers at Featherstone (Pontefract), where a miners' dispute was in progress. Mr. Asquith, who was then the Home Secretary, was charged with the responsibility for this attack on the workers, and was for a long time afterwards known as " Featherstone Asquith."

There were echoes at the Norwich Congress the following year over the Home Rule question, several little scenes took place, but the Congress, as such, did not associate itself with the opinions of either side.

A big sensation was caused at the Birmingham Congress when it was announced that one of the best-known titled ladies in the country, the Countess of Warwick, had openly joined and associated herself with the Labour Movement. This action of Lady Warwick's, I afterwards learnt, meant a great financial sacrifice to her, for King Edward, who was one of the trustees of her estate, curtailed the countess's income by a very substantial annual sum.

The countess invited the delegates to visit the castle as her guests. Since then Lady Warwick has taken an active part in the Labour Movement and has given her country house, Easton Lodge, Dunmow, Essex, for the use of the Labour Party.

Sir James O'Grady, who has just been appointed Governor of Tasmania, is a very old friend of mine. He presided at a Trade Union Congress at Bristol. At this Congress I was elected, with the late Mr. W. Inskip, to carry the fraternal greetings of the British Trade Union Congress to the Convention of the American Federation of Labour that was to be held in Kansas City, U.S.A.

Whenever I was in Bristol I used to stay at the house of our district secretary there, Mr. Harold Brabham. Brabham was always boasting about his ability as a cook.

One day, being rather tired of listening to these boasts, I said to him : " Well, I think I could cook a dinner as good as any one, meat and vegetables ; but I've never tried to make a plum pudding. Still, I'll bet you ten shillings that I'll cook as good a pudding as you can."

He accepted the bet. We sent for the ingredients, took two mixing bowls, and got to work. The puddings mixed, we put them in cloths, and then into boiling water, and sat down to await the results.

After the puddings had been boiled the right length of time, we took them out of the pot, and Brabham's pudding was " champion," as they say in Yorkshire ; but mine was as heavy as lead. I said no more about being able to cook as I handed Brabham the 10s. he had won from me.

Although I made a mess of cooking this pudding, I still consider myself a handy man about the kitchen, for in my early days, when my mother was compelled to go out to work, I often did the cooking for my brothers and sisters. Even to-day I often cook my own food at home. I would like to challenge my colleagues in the Labour Movement to a dinner-cooking contest, and I think I would get very near the first prize !

CHAPTER IX

ACROSS THE ATLANTIC

A GREAT adventure lay ahead of me. I had made several trips on the Continent ; but now I was to go farther afield, for the time had arrived for my trip to America, for which I was selected at the Bristol Conference, earlier in the year, with Mr. Inskip. We had a wonderful send-off from friends at London and Liverpool. Our ship for the journey across the Atlantic was the *Campania*, one of the largest boats afloat at the time.

We were only a few hours out from Liverpool when Mr. Inskip became seriously ill with hæmorrhage of the lungs. He was confined to his cabin for the whole of the journey, and I had to spend most of my time looking after him. We had a very rough passage across the Atlantic, and for two days the passengers were not allowed on deck. The ship had no " rolling logs " and she bobbed about like a cork.

During the journey I got into conversation with one of the passengers, a lace weaver from Nottingham, who had with him six girl lace makers. I learnt that an American employer, who had been in Nottingham, had engaged this man and the girls to work for him at his factory in one of the New England States of America. This was contrary to the law, for a heavy penalty is imposed by the American authorities on any one who contracts with workers in other countries to go to America to work.

The American authorities had received information about this party, and when we landed at New York the man and the girls were detained.

Six weeks later, when I came through New York again, I found these people still under detention. I visited the employer at his hotel, and told him that one of the girls was my sister. I told him several other things, too. We got into a very heated argument and almost came to blows. In the end he apologised, and assured me that the man and the girls would be well compensated for the trouble he had caused them.

I was very excited as I stood on the deck while the ship steamed towards New York harbour. I felt a thrill as we passed the great statue of Liberty, and was filled with awe by the skyline of New York, with its great skyscrapers and buildings packed close together like boxes and cases on end.

The late Mr. Samuel Gompers, President of the American Federation of Labour, had sent a tender to meet our ship, and the Customs authorities had been notified of our identity, so that we could pass through without the customary delay and inspection of our belongings.

Reporters, photographers, and a big crowd of friends met us on landing. I did not tell the reporters very much, when they asked me for an interview, but I afterwards read long and lurid stories in the newspapers of what I was supposed to have told them.

We were to learn very shortly how lavish American hospitality can be. The very first night in New York a great banquet had been arranged for us by the New York Civic Society. There must have been over a thousand people present, including prominent people in all walks of society. Mr. Gompers welcomed us in a cordial speech, to which I was asked to respond ; but I was so dead tired from travelling that I could only make a very brief reply.

I made up, however, for this semi-silence before I reached Kansas City, where the Convention we were attending was to be held. All along the thousand-mile route meetings had been arranged, at which we were expected to meet the local trade unionists and deliver speeches to them.

Our first stop was at Rochester, where lunch was waiting for us at one of the big hotels. I went into the dining-room alone and sat down, but I was never more embarrassed in my life than when the waiter brought me seven courses on a tray all at the same time. I sat and looked at this luxurious array of food, and puzzled my brain as to which course I should eat first. I looked round at the other diners for inspiration. After a little while I began to feel so uncomfortable that I got up and left. I was very glad to get out of that hotel, and for the rest of my trip I never took my meals alone.

I had an exciting time at another town. After speaking at a big meeting, a Mr. Tobin, with whom I was travelling, took me into an American public-house. They call them saloons, and there were men bartenders instead of barmaids. There were quite a number of people in the place at the time, when suddenly a fight started. We did not know what it was all about, but the two combatants were going at each other as hard as they could.

A bartender jumped over the counter, landed several punches on one of the men, and then rushed out of the place calling for a policeman.

He returned in a minute with the biggest policeman I have ever seen. He grabbed one of the men by the collar, gave him a push, and kicked him out of the place. Then he started to deal with the other man with his baton. It was brutal treatment.

I said to the policeman, " I think you are punishing the wrong man." He told me to mind my own business, adding : " If you don't both beat it I'll take you along with me." A word to the wise was sufficient, so we made ourselves scarce !

" I'm going to take you to see something you have never seen in your life, and probably will not see again." This threat was made to me by Mr. Tobin when we arrived in Buffalo. I was curious, and asked him what it was, but his answer was the same as that of Mr. Asquith on a certain well-known occasion, " Wait and see." We jumped on one of the single-decker street cars and rode to a big restaurant. To get into the place we had to go down a passage that was only about four feet wide. " Here you are," said Tobin. " Look at this ! " He was pointing to the floor, and I saw to my astonishment that it was paved with American coins, from a nickel up to twenty-dollar gold pieces. Tobin told me that this place was unique, there being no other such place in America.

I noticed that the whisky bottle was put on the counter and that the customers helped themselves. On one occasion I saw a man in a saloon take more than one nip, and the bartender asked him, sarcastically, if he was going to drown himself.

The great Niagara Falls are near Buffalo. I had often wanted to see them, so I took this opportunity. It was a wonderful experience. I found that I could go right under the Falls. To do this I had to put on an oilskin coat and go down in a lift. When right down under the Falls I looked out and saw enormous volumes of water roaring, splashing and spouting in front of me as it tore along, forming whirlpools of terrific speed and activity. Part of the Falls are on the Canadian side of the border, and part on the American side. I thought the Canadian side the prettier. It was winter time, and very cold, and at Goats Island, on the American side, the spray formed into icicles. It looked like a fairy palace that one only sees in happy dreams.

Before I left the Falls I had an adventure as a smuggler. While on the Canadian side I found that furs could be bought very cheaply, so I bought one for my wife. It was much cheaper than I could have bought in England or in the United States. There was a heavy tax on furs going into America and as we had to cross the big steel bridge to get back to Buffalo I was rather worried as to how to get the fur through without paying duty.

Tobin solved the problem by hiring a two-horse four-wheeled carriage. The Customs officer on the Canadian side was not concerned with goods going out of the country, and we passed him without a hitch, but when we got to the American side we ran into trouble. The American Customs officer wanted to make a thorough search of the carriage and of our persons. Things looked black for a moment, until Tobin took the officer aside and told him that I was one of the Fraternal Delegates from England to the American Federation of Labour. When he heard this he let us pass without further inspection, thus enabling me to smuggle my fur through.

The windy city of Chicago was the next place we stopped at. It was a sharp frosty morning, and my nose and ears tingled with the cold. Here, like every other place we stopped at, great hospitality and a grand welcome were given us. In the evening a big social and dance was held in our honour, and here I saw, for the first time, the famous cake walk danced. It was a competition for the best two cake-walkers, and it was won by a boy and girl of about sixteen years of age.

While in Chicago I was taken on a visit to the packing houses, where thousands of cattle, pigs, and poultry are killed, dressed, and packed daily. These abattoirs and meat works cover a great area, and the odour thereof is great. I saw the cattle being killed and going through the various processes of dressing and packing ; not a very savoury sight.

The Spanish-American War had just ended while I was in Chicago, and one of the American generals who had played a prominent part in the struggle had just returned home to Chicago. A reception was given in his honour at which over 2,000 women and girls kissed the general. Because of this incident, he received the unofficial title of " The Kissing General."

A convention of the American Federation of Labour is a much more exciting affair than a British Trade Union Congress. There are more delegates. The procedure is different, and much more vigour is used by the delegates, both in expressing their opinions and in applauding or deriding the opinions of others. Often the proceedings were held up for a short time by singing or shouting in chorus. There were so many passionate and exciting scenes that I soon realised that this was just the ordinary way the delegates had of approving, or disapproving, of any proposition. During one of the debates a question of nationalisation was discussed, and both Mr. Inskip and myself were invited to vote on the question. A good deal of laughter was caused when Mr. Inskip voted against the proposal, and I voted for it.

Mr. Gompers, president, asked me to preside over the Congress for a few hours. After seeing how excited the delegates got, I was rather timid about accepting the invitation. I tackled the task, and handled the delegates well, but I think they were on their best behaviour while I was in the chair.

There was quite a local sensation while we were in Kansas City as a result of the custom of the local authorities in making a levy on the rates for the purpose of carrying out the work of the town from January to December of each year. It was the middle of December, and all the money had been spent. There was not even sufficient funds in hand to pay the workmen or the officials of the town, nor would there be until the end of the year. This caused a slight political upheaval and gave us a good insight into the method of American municipal administration.

Kansas City, like Chicago, is also a great meat packing centre. The residents of the city are very proud of their works, and we were invited to visit them. I saw something here that I did not see at the Chicago works. Pigs, after being killed, were passed through boiling water and scalded, and were afterwards taken to another floor, where niggers scraped and dressed them. This room was so full of steam that I had great difficulty in seeing the men. I was told that the work was so unpleasant that only coloured men could be secured to do it.

In the slaughter-house I saw cattle being pushed into a narrow gangway. At the end of the gangway were the killers, armed with hatchets, with which they hit the bullocks on the head as they passed. As they were hit they fell and slid down a chute. At the bottom of the chute their four legs were tied and the carcasses hanged on a moving chain. Along this chain butchers were stationed, and they dressed the carcasses as they passed. It was a revolting sight. The butchers were a mass of blood, and the odour was not at all pleasant.

The floors in this room were made of concrete, and the blood which was drained off ran into a basement, where it was filtered and made ready for use as " black puddings " and for other purposes. I was told that over two thousand animals had been killed that day. It was a sight that has left a distinct mark on my memory by its gruesomeness.

Before the Congress was over, both Inskip and myself made speeches to the delegates in which we conveyed the fraternal greetings of the British Trade Union Movement.

During the Congress week one of the delegates came to me and said, " Thorne, can you tell me the time ? " I pulled out my old silver watch and told him, and never thought any more of the incident ; but on the last day of the Congress I was presented with a very fine gold watch, engraved with my name and the occasion on which it was presented. Inskip was presented with a gold-mounted walking stick. I still wear my watch, and it reminds me of the fine experience I had in America.

On the homeward journey we did not stop at towns along the way, but had several days and nights on the train. We had a first-class sleeper. Mine was the top bunk, and below me, to my surprise, a lady was sleeping. I had to use a small ladder to get into my bunk. I said to Sam Gompers, " This is rather strange, a woman is sleeping in the bunk below mine." He said, " Oh, no, that's all right, it's the custom to let the women have the bottom bunk ; it saves them climbing up the ladder."

One night on the train we went very deeply into the question of rye whisky. We consumed quite a quantity of it. At bedtime, Jimmy Duncan, one of the vice-presidents of the Federation, said to me : " Thorne, you'll never be able to walk straight to your bunk to-night." The rye whisky had given me a lot of confidence in myself, and I said, " You come and see ; I will walk to my bunk as straight as a gun barrel." I made a good passage, and lay in my bunk until the morning, but in my sleep I saw many wonderful things. I've often tried to get rye whisky in this country !

At Washington, which is not in any State (but is called the District of Columbia, and the seat of the American Federal Government), we visited the Congressional Library, one of the most beautiful buildings I have ever seen. Inside we went up to the Whispering Gallery, where the slightest sound may be heard.

We also visited the White House, the residence of the President of the United States. I noticed that streets radiated in all directions from this building, and I was told that, in the event of riots, every avenue was protected by guns of different calibre. While in Washington, Mr. Gompers entertained us at the Hotel Raleigh, the finest hotel in the city, and the most luxurious I have ever been in. This was before America went dry, and we did justice to the hotel's best champagne.

I had a wonderful time in America. As well as being a duty it was a real pleasure, and the first holiday worthy of the name that I had enjoyed for a number of years. I lived very well during the trip; but the hospitality of the Americans must be blamed, and not my own desires, for I am a man of simple tastes.

CHAPTER X

ODD EXPERIENCES

BACK in dear old England again I was elected to attend the Trade Union Congress that was held at Plymouth. I have a very sad memory of this Congress, because of the report that was received that my dear friend and companion on my American trip, Mr. Inskip, had died.

This was the first Congress that Miss Margaret Bondfield, the first woman to hold high Government office, attended. The question of child labour was one of the issues raised at this Congress. A resolution was discussed protesting against the British Empire being built on children's hearts, and money made out of children's wasted lives. David Shackelton (now Sir David Shackelton), who holds an important permanent Government position, opposed this resolution, which was, however, carried by an overwhelming majority. Compulsory arbitration of industrial disputes, which is again being suggested by leaders of industry, was rejected at the Congress.

The Congress was made historic by the carrying of a resolution instructing the Parliamentary Committee to convene a special conference for the purpose of inaugurating a great united Labour Party. This meeting, which I took part in, was held at the Memorial Hall, London. Mr. Ramsay MacDonald (the first Labour Prime Minister of Great Britain) was elected the first secretary of what has grown to be the second largest political party in the country.

I often made trips to Ireland to do organising work for the union. On one of these visits I had arranged to hold a meeting at Wexford. When I arrived at the hall I found inside several members of the Royal Irish Constabulary. It was a new experience to me to have policemen attending and taking notes of a trade union meeting, so I asked them what they were doing inside the hall. They told me to mind my own business, and that I would find members of the constabulary at every meeting I held in Southern Ireland.

On this trip I visited Cork. Our branch secretary, Joe O'Gorman, one of the best Irishmen I have ever seen, met me there. Every year on St. Patrick's Day he sends me a box of shamrock. He asked me to go with him to Blarney, and invited me to try to kiss the Blarney Stone. I said I would like to see the stone, but that kissing it was another matter.

When we got to the stone I found that it was down a deep pit, and that if you wanted to kiss it some one would have to hold your legs while you tried.

When I saw the distance I should fall if the people holding my legs let go their hold, I said to Joe, " No, thank you ; I'd rather kiss a woman than that stone ! "

I watched several people kiss the stone, which I thought was an extraordinary business, especially as the people had to be held upside down to do it.

Odd experiences have often come my way. For a very short while I was a director of a newspaper.

One of the big strikes in the mining industry was in progress and I was talking with a few friends about the lack of news from the miners' point of view that was being published in the daily papers. I suggested we should start a newspaper, both for the purpose of stating the miners' case and as a means of appealing for funds to help them in their struggle.

With this idea in my mind I got together a number of friends. We formed a board of directors, and started a paper. But like many another journalistic enterprise, we could not carry on because of our slender resources, which were soon exhausted; even Labour papers with willing and voluntary workers need capital as well as enthusiasm.

This was my first and last experience as a promoter of a company and a director of a newspaper. It was a sad experience, but I had the satisfaction of knowing that the money we had lost was lost in a good cause.

Others have been more successful with newspapers. Robert Blatchford was one of these fortunate people. When he was editing the *Clarion* I asked him to address a meeting for me. He told me it was the first trade union meeting at which he had ever spoken, and although the meeting was well advertised there was a very poor attendance.

About this meeting and Blatchford, I will only say that, in my opinion, he has been a better writer than a public speaker.

Much of my own public speaking has been done on behalf of the unemployed, and my activities starting many, many years ago in this work have brought me both roses and thorns.

From the dock gates in the crowded East End, with all the leaders and my old colleagues of the time, we stirred the starving unemployed to cry for bread. Their plaintive cry was heard by some.

The *Daily News* sent C. F. Masterman as a special commissioner into the East End, and his able pen was responsible for many pathetic appeals that appeared in that paper.

Jack Jones, M.P., and Arthur Hayday, M.P., and the Rev. George Hooper were all in this bitter fight against poverty, and as a result of their efforts money, food and clothing came to relieve the suffering.

There were no fewer than 10,000 people unemployed in my own borough of West Ham. Their condition was appalling. Mr. Arnold Hill, the managing director of the Thames Iron Works, offered to grant the town council £1,000 for the purpose of starting relief work in the borough, but his £1,000 was hedged round with the condition that the men employed on such work should only receive 4*d*. per hour for six hours a day and for four days a week.

I protested against this, because the rate suggested was 2*d*. less than the trade union rate, but in spite of my opposition the resolution was carried. I organised a mass meeting of the unemployed, and a huge crowd turned up at Beckton Road corner.

The meeting appointed a deputation to wait on the next town council meeting. The deputation marched from Beckton Road corner to the Stratford Town Hall, where the council was sitting. The deputation was accompanied by large crowds of the unemployed, and when they arrived I left the council chamber and appealed to the people not to come into conflict with the police, large numbers of whom were on special duty.

I introduced the deputation to the council. It was a remarkable deputation. The leader carried a red flag, and for the first time to my knowledge this emblem of the workers wa displayed in such an austere and dignified place.

The agitation was successful and trade union rates of wages and conditions were observed on all relief work that was carried out. I received a large number of letters, and many more were printed in the *Stratford Express*, thanking me and approving my action in the matter.

I made the acquaintance of the dock at Bow Street Police Court in my activities on behalf of the unemployed. This came about when I addressed a meeting I had arranged in Trafalgar Square. The day before my meeting Miss Christabel Pankhurst had held a demonstration in connection with the fight for woman's suffrage. Her speech was what might be termed " violent," for she declared that the women were going to rush the House of Commons on the following Monday.

In my speech I referred to Miss Pankhurst's remarks and suggested that it would be futile to assail the Houses of Parliament, as there was nothing in them worth the trouble. I told the crowd, " If your wives and children are hungry, the best thing to do is to rush the bakers' shops ! "

Miss Pankhurst's speech resulted in her being summoned to Bow Street, and while in the dock she asked the Chief Inspector if he had heard Will Thorne's speech on the day following her own ; and if so, she wanted to know why Will Thorne was not in the dock with her.

Until I heard of this I had not realised that in my excitement I had made a rather dangerous statement. Even then I did not think it was serious. But when Lord Robert Cecil asked the Attorney-General in the House of Commons whether his attention had been called to the language I had used in Trafalgar Square, and whether legal action was to be taken, I realised that there might be serious consequences arising from my utterances. There were. The Commissioner of Police summoned me to appear before the magistrate, who, by the way, was H. Curtis Bennett, and I was charged with being—

" Guilty of conduct likely to provoke a breach of the peace by advising and inciting in the course of a public speech the members of the unemployed to do a certain illegal act namely to rush every baker's shop in London rather than starve."

The penalty for committing such a crime as this was, I believe, seven years imprisonment with hard labour.

I duly appeared at Bow Street to answer the charge. Mr. Pete Curran, M.P., Mr. J. R. Clynes, M.P., and Mr. J. O'Grady, M.P. (now Sir James O'Grady, Governor of Tasmania), went with me to the court. Mr. Muskett, who prosecuted, said the authorities regarded the case as of the utmost importance. I was not at all nervous

as I stood in the dock facing the stern administrators of
the law and my accusers. I defended myself.

I asked the main witness, Police-Sergeant Abbott, of
Scotland Yard, whether he had ever reported speeches
in Trafalgar Square. He said he had not. I asked him
how many words a minute he could take in shorthand,
and he said " from one hundred and forty to one hundred and fifty."

He admitted that I spoke very rapidly and that he
was pressed in by a crowd. He also admitted that he
did not take down everything I said, but only what he
considered inflammatory. I asked him if he heard me
say the words on which the charge was based and he
admitted that he did not. I caused a flutter of laughter
in the court when I suggested that he only took down
the " tit-bits."

After further evidence I made it clear to the court
that my conduct had not, nor was it likely to, cause the
illegal actions that the law feared.

I asked for an adjournment for a week for the purpose of engaging counsel, but this was not necessary,
for the magistrate bound me over to keep the peace in
two sureties of £50 each from Pete Curran and James
O'Grady, and myself in one surety of £100.

After this affair I did not give up addressing meetings, and every Friday night in the House of Commons
O'Grady would make it a point to see me. His usual
plea was, " For Heaven's sake, Thorne, be careful what
you say, if you don't I'll have to sell up my home to
find the fifty pounds, and I don't believe I've got fifty
pound's worth of furniture in it ! "

I got a certain amount of fun out of this, and used to
pull O'Grady's leg by telling him that if he lost his £50
I would lose £100, and if my furniture had to be sold it
would not realise half that amount. I continued my
speaking, however, and though I sailed near the wind I
managed to keep within the law.

While I was attending at Bow Street Mr. Victor
Grayson was creating a scene in the House of Commons

on the same subject that had got me into the dock. He had told me that he was determined to get Parliament to deal with the urgent question of unemployment. " If they don't," he said, " I'm going to cause trouble, even if it means me getting thrown out."

What happened was that just after 2.30 o'clock, looking pale and moody, Grayson entered the House and took his seat in the Labour benches. He sat with his green Tyrolese hat pulled low over his forehead, listening with gloomy expression to the debate.

Ten minutes later he was a different man. Young, defiant, his face flushed with excitement, his hands clasped firmly behind his back, his shoulders squared to the assembly, and regardless of all decorum, he poured his resonant musical voice into the chamber.

" Mr. Chairman, Mr. Chairman," he shouted. " Before you proceed any further——"

The cry of " Order, order," came from every corner of the chamber, but, shouting loudly above the din, Grayson continued. " Thousands of people are starving in the streets while you are proceeding with this Bill."

Waving his hands with excitement, the Chairman (the House was in Committee) stood calling for order. But Grayson was not to be silenced. He was growing more excited. " I absolutely refuse to give order ! " he shouted. " I refuse to allow the House to proceed while I am in it."

The whole chamber was in uproar. Cries of " Sit down ! " and " Order ! " were flung from every side and every corner. The Chairman tried to explain that, as the House was in Committee, no motion could be put forward. Grayson would not listen, he would not sit down, he would not obey the order of the Chair ; he declared that he felt so deeply that he must refuse to obey the rules. He continued in his refusal to sit down or to withdraw from the chamber, and he was finally removed by force.

My early days of hunger, and the poverty I endured, left their mark upon me. It is perhaps because of this that, in all my activities, I have kept the question of the unemployed in the forefront of my work.

From the days of my first arrival in West Ham I have taken a keen interest in the municipal government of the borough. In those days what is now the Barking Road had not been made, and I remember that the carts and waggons taking produce to the City often sank down to the axles in the soft, marshy ground.

My first municipal election took place in November, 1891, when I was elected with a big majority over my opponent, the manager of a large factory at Silvertown. In those days I was considered a very revolutionary character because I was advocating public baths and wash-houses, and municipally-owned trams!

As a member of the S.D.F., I had to sign a declaration form. I have a copy of it in front of me now, and it reads as follows :—

" I, William Thorne, hereby pledge myself to work for the objects in the programme of the S.D.F. if elected to the Town Council for the Borough of West Ham, and also to submit to the guidance of the Canning Town Branch on all questions concerning my actions and votes on the Town Council, and I further pledge myself to withdraw from the Town Council if requested to do so by a special meeting of the Branch or Branches summoned according to rule.

(*Signed*) " WILLIAM JAMES THORNE.
" *November 3rd,* 1891."

I had no objection to signing this declaration, although I thought it was unnecessary in my case, for if a man has real genuine intentions of doing work to help his fellow-men, as I did, such a declaration is unnecessary.

In those days, after a municipal election, the Mayor used to invite the aldermen and councillors to luncheon to talk over municipal matters, and to congratulate each other on their election. I refused to attend this function.

One of the first things I noticed was that the landlords and rent collectors would always fight very hard to get on the Public Health Committee. The reason for this was that this committee controlled the sanitary inspector, who visited houses for the purpose of reporting to the medical officer, who in turn reported to the Health Committee for the purpose of enforcing landlords to keep their properties in a sanitary and healthy state of repair. With the committee packed with small property owners and rent collectors, these prosecutions were reduced to a minimum.

I was the first Labour and Socialist member, as such, to be elected to the Council for a number of years, but now we have over forty members on the Council, and a clear majority over the other parties.

A rather funny incident occurred when I was nominated for the mayoralty. At a private meeting, I learned that one of my own colleagues objected to me and refused to vote for me because he said he had heard that I would refuse to wear the mayoral robes if elected. I was not elected, however, being beaten by three votes. My turn came later, when I was elected Deputy Mayor in 1899, Alderman in 1910, and Mayor in 1917–18. I am at present an alderman, and will remain one until 1926.

During these thirty-three years of municipal work I have had a long strenuous uphill fight, but I have the satisfaction of knowing that I have the entire confidence of the majority of the people and of my colleagues in West Ham. During that time I have had some interesting municipal experiences. One of these was in 1913, when I received the following letter in connection with the visit of the King to open a new reservoir. The letter was from the town clerk, and said :—

" DEAR MR. ALDERMAN,—
       " It is suggested from Buckingham Palace that you and Sir John Bethell, as representatives in Parliament of the Borough, should be on the platform to be

introduced to His Majesty on Saturday, and the Mayor would be glad to know whether it would be convenient for you to fall in with this arrangement. A reply by return will oblige.

> " I am, dear Mr. Alderman,
> " Yours faithfully,
> (*Signed*) " FRED. E. HILLEARY."

My reply to this letter caused quite a sensation. I will give it in full. This is what I wrote :—

" DEAR MR. TOWN CLERK,—

" Your letter of the 12th inst. duly to hand, for which I am much obliged, in which it is suggested from Buckingham Palace that Sir John Bethell and myself, as representatives of the Borough, should be on the platform to be introduced to His Majesty on Saturday. I am very much obliged to the chief officials of Buckingham Palace for the honour suggested, and I sincerely hope that they will not think me in any way discourteous by declining the invitation. I quite recognise that the opening of a new waterworks reservoir by Their Majesties means a great deal more to the East London people than they perhaps recognise. If I thought that by Their Majesties coming through the East of London and receiving an address of welcome at Stratford would in any way be a means of mitigating the deep-rooted and chronic poverty in the Borough, I should then feel it a pleasure to be on the platform and accept the invitation. My principles and views on these matters have been known for many years.

" I sincerely hope that the day will be fine and that Their Majesties will have a safe and pleasant journey coming and returning.

" Thanking both yourself and the Mayor for the honour intended,

> " I am, dear sir,
> " Yours sincerely,
> (*Signed*) " WILL THORNE."

I earned the displeasure of many people on account of this refusal to meet the King, but I also received the congratulations of many more people because of the reasons that actuated me in doing what I did.

Again the question of unemployment was to get me into trouble. I was served with a surcharge notice and requested to attend at the Educational Offices, Stratford, to show cause why I should not repay £130 7s. 3d., part of the cost of meals and food supplied to necessitous children during periods when schools were closed, at Easter, May Day, Whitsun, Mid-Term, and Christmas.

I refused to attend, and from that day to this I have never paid the money, nor do I intend to. I told the authorities that they knew my address, and that if they wanted the £130 they could come along and take my goods and chattels, then worth about £60. I have never heard any more about the matter.

I refused to pay this surcharge because I believed that we who were responsible for spending the money were justified in feeding the starving children. At the time this took place many recollections passed through my mind of the hungry times I had as a boy, and how often I had sat round the table at home on a Sunday—a dinner table with no dinner on it.

I atoned in the minds of some people for my previous discourtesy to the King, when during the war I suggested that the King and Queen might care to visit the hospital at Whipps' Cross. The suggestion was adopted, and I accompanied their majesties on their visit. A few days afterwards I received the following letter from Buckingham Palace, signed by Lord Stamfordham :—

" DEAR MR. THORNE,
    " The King wishes me to tell you how glad he and the Queen are to have carried out their visit to Whipps' Cross Hospital as originally suggested by you. His Majesty was also pleased to see you again

and in the earliest days of your Mayoralty of West Ham.

" Their Majesties were made gratified by the hearty welcome given to them by the large crowd in the streets through which they passed.

" Believe me,

" Yours very truly,

" STAMFORDHAM."

As the Mayor of the Borough I thanked the King and Queen for the honour they had paid by their visit to the hospital. While the Queen was busy presenting gifts, I was having a rather vigorous talk with the King. I was particularly keen to let him know as much as I possibly could about the terrible poverty of the people. He took a great interest in what I had to say, and the questions he asked made me realise that his was not a formal interest, but a real desire to know the conditions of his subjects.

I must have got carried away by my subject, as it appears I was talking quite loudly, for the Queen turned round and said, " This is not the time for talk," and so the King and I had to end our interesting conversation.

I had a busy year as Mayor. I collected over £40,000 for the erection of a war memorial in West Ham. I knew that a monument of stone would be of no practical use to the people of the borough, and my suggestion that the memorial should take the form of an out-patient department to the Queen Mary's Hospital was adopted as the best way of spending the money, and of showing that we remembered the boys killed and wounded in the war. I laid the foundation stone of the building last year, and this year, on Armistice Day, H.R.H. Prince Henry, who is President of the Hospital, formally opened the building.

It was no easy job to collect such a large sum as £40,000. I am afraid I made myself somewhat of a nuisance in doing it. I visited all the managers, managing directors, and shareholders of the big factories, breweries, and other large works in the borough, and asked them for their contributions, and although they were opposed to my politics they subscribed very generously.

Many of them were surprised to see me; they told me they had heard and read a lot about me and thought I was a very dangerous man; but I explained to them that I was not nearly the ferocious animal some people made me out to be.

I have seen many of my ambitions realised in West Ham. One of these is the establishment of a technical institute, built mainly with money obtained from a tax on whisky; and several other institutions, including the fever hospital, which was built by direct labour as a partial result of my efforts.

In all my activities, municipal, parliamentary, and trade union—and even in my social and personal life—the problem of unemployment has always obtruded itself. From the earliest days of the union, as I go through the records, this problem has always been present. Year after year, behind the figures of the financial toll on the union, are numerous tragedies of hunger and want.

Unemployment has cost the union a great amount of money; but even larger amounts have been spent on strikes and lock-outs which were caused either directly or indirectly by the conditions that prevailed during fluctuations in trade.

One such dispute was the great engineers' lock-out, when a weekly levy of 3d. per member was made in all the engineering and allied trades. This was a disastrous dispute to all the trade unions in the country, and ended in Colonel Dyer (the employers' leader) imposing a five years' agreement on the engineers, from which it took many more years to recover.

This war of the classes, the never-ending struggle between those who have and those who have not, in which I have tried to play my part in the interests of my class—the workers—has meant for me an almost unending succession of strikes and disputes. I have been engaged in so many struggles that I find it impossible to enumerate them. Some, however, are more vivid in my memory than others.

One of these big strikes was at the Gas Works in Llanelly. In this dispute I came in contact with a notorious strike breaker, who was paid so much per head for supplying blackleg labour. The strike lasted only a little more than a week, and arose through the manager of the works refusing to recognise a system of seniority of service, a system that was in operation in most of the gas works of the country.

On the second night of the strike the greater part of the town was in darkness. The theatres were closed and many works were shut down. The manager assured the townspeople that there would shortly be a plentiful supply of gas, as he had arranged for men to take the strikers' place ; but, after a few days he was only able to secure two men, who were locked inside the works and guarded by a large body of policemen.

During the week the number of blacklegs was increased, but they were unable to maintain a supply of gas sufficient for the illumination of the town. When I arrived in the town it was in darkness. At the station thousands of people had gathered to welcome me. They were singing " We will hang Old —— on a Sour Apple Tree," referring to the manager. The song was being sung both in Welsh and English.

I found that a lot of damage had been done in the town. Windows had been smashed and other damage done, and a lot of people were arrested. A large number of police were also in evidence.

After a few days' negotiation I managed to arrange a settlement ; the blacklegs were cleared out, and their leader had to be compensated. Though the strike cost the union £8,000 it was a victory, and the manager who was responsible for it was afterwards cleared out of the company.

The blast furnaces at Ilkeston were also the scene of

several strikes, and on one of my visits to this town a
member asked me if I had ever seen Ernest Terah
Hooley, the notorious financier, who is at present writing his sensational confessions. I said, " No ; why ? "

" Well," he said, " he is a very interesting person,
and a man who has taken a good deal of interest in the
Labour Movement. I think he is anxious to become a
Parliamentary candidate, and if you like I'll get you an
introduction to him."

I told my friend that I would like to meet him, that I
had read a great deal about him in the papers and of
the way he had been distributing his money in Ilkeston.
Then I remembered that I had heard of a similar man
before, and asked my friend what he was.

" I believe he is connected with big commercial companies."

I told my friend : " If you mean he is a company
promoter, I don't want to see Mr. Hooley, or any one
else connected with that kind of business."

I never thought at that time that Mr. Hooley would
go to gaol as a result of the activities by which he
swindled many people.

Shortly after this we had another strike at Derby,
where I organised the strikers to use more than peaceful persuasion. My methods won the strike. One of
the men, not directly affected by the dispute, whose
wife kept a public-house, the " Locomotive Inn," came
out in sympathy with the strikers, with the result that
his wife turned him out of his home. I met him some
little time after completely " down and out " and
helped him as best I could.

These disputes were often the subject of lively discussions at Trade Union Congresses, and more than one
such matter was raised at the Glasgow Congress. It was
at this Congress that Keir Hardie, with his determination to push for Independent Labour Party representation, called a number of delegates together, including
myself and J. Havelock Wilson.

He was very anxious to start an organisation for

Independent Parliamentary representation of Labour, to break all connections with Liberals and Tories, and form a distinct Labour Party in the House of Commons. While I thought this would be a very good thing I had to remind my friend Hardie that I had been a member of the Social Democratic Federation for over eight years, and I could not see my way clear to become one of the promoters of the I.L.P. The first conference of the I.L.P. was held later at Bradford, and I was elected to attend it. At this conference I met for the first time Mr. Philip Snowden, who became the first Labour Chancellor of the Exchequer.

What was more important than the foundation of the I.L.P.—the formation of the Labour Party—took place in London in February, 1900. This arose from a resolution at the previous Trade Union Congress at Plymouth, where the Parliamentary Committee of the Congress, of which I was a member, was instructed to convene a conference of representatives of trade unions, co-operative societies and socialist bodies to discuss the question of Labour representation in the House of Commons.

At this Conference 129 delegates, representing over half a million members, were present. Mr. J. Ramsay Macdonald acted as honorary secretary of the committee which had been appointed to make the preparations. I was the representative of the Parliamentary Committee of the Trade Union Congress ; Keir Hardie and Ramsay MacDonald represented the I.L.P. ; Harry Quelch the S.D.F. ; and Bernard Shaw the Fabian Society.

I had the pleasure of moving that Mr. W. T. Steadman, M.P., be elected chairman of the Conference, and this was carried unanimously. J. R. Clynes, now the Right Honourable, was elected one of the tellers, and Pete Curran, also an official of my union, topped the poll in the election for the Standing Orders Committee.

A large number of resolutions were on the agenda for discussion. One of these on " Working-class Represen-

tatives " was moved by George Barnes (now the Right
Honourable), who represented the engineers, and this
was seconded by John Burns, M.P., who said, among
other things in his speech, that he " was tired of working-class boots, working-class trams, working-class
houses and working-class margarine."

When Jimmy MacDonald, of the S.D.F., moved a
resolution for a Labour Party in Parliament, two
amendments were moved by delegate Wilkie, of the
Shipwrights, and Keir Hardie. Eventually, Keir
Hardie's amendment became the main motion, which
was supported by Jack Burns, who said there was a distinct Labour Party in Parliament, Mr. Sam Woods and
himself being Whips. They did not call themselves
independent ; they had not worn Trilby hats and red
ties, but they had done the work, and he warned them
against too much dictation.

I reminded friend Burns that he had worn the red tie,
and at an early stage of the movement in the '80's had
thought about red ties and flags, and it seemed as if he
had now turned a complete somersault. Eventually,
however, Hardie's amendment was carried unanimously.

At the election of officers of the first Labour Representation Committee, Mr. Ramsay MacDonald was
unanimously elected the first secretary. Little did I
think at that time that he would one day become
Prime Minister of Great Britain.

It gives me great satisfaction to know that I was one
of the founders of the organisation that has developed
into the present great National Labour Party, and that
I have attended every annual meeting since then, including the one held at Queen's Hall, London, on
October 27, 1924, when Ramsay MacDonald, as Prime
Minister, made his famous speech on the Dissolution of
the first Labour Government.

The highest honour in the Trade Union movement
was conferred upon me at Newport in 1912, when I was
appointed president of the Trade Union Congress held

there in September of that year. My punctuality in starting the proceedings, and in carrying them on, earned me an additional title to that of president. I was called the " Little Tsar " by many of the delegates. It was a very successful Congress, representative of over two million organised trade unionists. During the preceding twelve months a strike of railway men, transport workers and dockers had taken place, and I was able to tell the Congress in my presidential address of the support and solidarity that was given to these workers by the rest of the movement.

At this Congress I was elected as the first Fraternal Delegate to the Canadian Labour Congress, and I have many pleasant recollections of that visit. Just nearing Quebec I saw on the riverside from the boat thousands of people gathered together, and I learnt that this was the annual celebration in memory of Joan of Arc. I only got a bird's eye view of the celebration, but I have never heard sweeter music than that which floated up to our ship from these thousands of people, who, like a massed choir, were singing sacred music.

I conveyed fraternal greetings to the Congress, and was presented with a diamond ring as a memento of the occasion. I have this ring locked away, and never wear it, for I am afraid that many of my members, who do not know that I was presented with it, might think it too luxurious for the secretary of a general labourers' union to wear !

Unlimited hospitality was extended to me by the Canadians. I must have been at least a stone heavier when I sailed for England again as a result of Canadian hospitality. One day, while out walking with one of the delegates, I noticed a big crowd near the river edge. I suggested to my companion that we might go and see what was happening, and when we reached the water side we were told that a sect known as the " Christian Endeavourers " were performing one of their ceremonies. Two men were standing in the water up to their arm-pits. Another man came and spoke to them, and they plunged themselves into the water. He spoke again, and they jumped out of the water and dashed away. Both men and women, though it was a bitterly cold day, took part in this strange ritual.

Before I left Canada I was treated to a wonderful meal in which " clam chowder," porter-house steaks (the largest I have ever seen), and champagne took a leading part in the menu.

CHAPTER XI

My trip to Canada was my longest journey, until I was asked by the Coalition Government to accompany a Labour delegation to Russia. G. H. Roberts was deputed by Mr. Lloyd George, then the Prime Minister, to ask me whether I was prepared to take the risk involved in this trip. I was told that my companions would be Jimmy O'Grady and W. S. Sanders. I agreed to go.

Arrangements were made and a date fixed for our departure. I had to leave King's Cross Station by the ten o'clock train for Aberdeen, so I left the House of Commons about five o'clock in the afternoon to go home for my luggage. As I was passing through the subway which leads from the Houses of Parliament to Westminster Underground Railway Station, I met F. E. Smith, now Lord Birkenhead, Secretary of State for India.

" Hullo, Thorne," he said. " I've been reading about you going to Russia as a delegate."

I told him that it was true. I noticed that he was wearing a fur coat with massive collar and cuffs.

" Well, Thorne, do you know it's very cold out there ? " he said.

I told him I had never been there before, and I only knew what I had read about Russia.

" Oh," he said, " you'd better take this coat with you ! " And he started to take it off.

I said I didn't think it would fit me ; but he told me to try it on, and it fitted me perfectly. I thanked him very much for his kindness, and promised to return the coat if I ever came home again.

I had only gone a few yards along the subway when I ran into one of my Labour colleagues, who looked at my magnificent overcoat with open-eyed astonishment. He asked me where I was going and whose coat I had on. I told him that I was going to Russia and that F. E. Smith had lent me the coat.

I was told afterwards that when he got to the House of Commons he informed people : " Thorne has joined the capitalist class ! I've just seen him wearing an overcoat that must have cost a few hundred pounds ! "

When I reached the station it was the rush hour, and I got into a third-class carriage. I was conscious that all eyes were upon me and my gorgeous coat, and I was thankful when I reached Upton Park and was able to leave the train. When I arrived home, my coat caused more surprise, and my wife told me that my colleagues would certainly make the coat the cause of jokes at my expense. She was right.

When I arrived at King's Cross Station, O'Grady greeted me with loud laughter and asked me, " Where did you get that —— coat from ? " When I told him, he said, " Well, you've got a darned cheek ! " I think he was only jealous of my comfort !

We took a Russian translator with us when we boarded the ship at Aberdeen, but the captain would not tell us exactly when the boat was going to sail. I said to O'Grady that this seemed rather a strange procedure, and he told me that the Newcastle to Norway route had been closed on account of so many boats being torpedoed by the German submarines. I remarked that, " It looks as though we're in for a rough time."

We went to our cabin, and when we awoke in the morning the ship was at sea. Our first stop was Bergen, in Norway, where we were shadowed by two men. On the way to Stockholm I saw that these two men were still keeping us under observation, so I said to O'Grady : " Those two fellows are still following us about, and I'm going to talk to them."

I went up to them and asked them why they were

following us. They said they were not. I then said I
did not believe them, and that if they continued
following us I would flatten them out. We saw no
more of them until the homeward journey, when they
again picked us up at Stockholm. I have since learnt
that they were two of the expensive and unnecessary
Secret Service agents maintained by our Government !

It was an interesting trip through Russia to Petrograd (now named Leningrad), where we stayed at a
very fine and large hotel. Arrangements had been made
for us to visit the Workmen's and Soldiers' Council,
which had been set up by the soldiers and sailors. We
expected that the Council would consist of many of
their representatives, but we were surprised to find that
nearly all the members were intellectuals who had been
selected from various parts of the Russian Empire. We
told them that we were delegates who brought fraternal
greetings of the British Government, and to wish them
success in their political revolution.

A few days later we met at the Duma what was known
as the " Three Thousand." These were 3,000 men and
women who had been selected to represent both the
various sections of the industrial working-class movement and the rank and file of the military and other
fighting forces. This reception took place in a very
large hall. It was a most interesting experience. The
place was well guarded, both inside and out, by soldiers,
fully armed with rifles and ammunition. There were
scenes of wild excitement and enthusiasm after we had
spoken to them and told them what the British people
were doing in the war, and when we conveyed fraternal
greetings from Britain.

While in Petrograd we visited, at the invitation of
the military officials, the barracks a little way out of
the town, where I met and had a long conversation
with the officer and the soldier who marked the
beginning of the revolution by their action in refusing
to shoot down the people. This action was as a signal
to the whole of the army, the navy and the workers.

In Russia we attended many meetings, and carried out detailed investigations, during which we came in contact with all the most important people in the country.   In Moscow we met a lawyer, who was a very close friend of Kerensky.   He told us the way in which the Tsar's Government had absolutely neglected to provide the army with munitions for carrying on the war.   We had proof of this when we visited several of the munition factories, which we found working at top speed.   The factories were controlled by a Workmen's Committee drawn from the workers on different sections of the task.   Members of the committee told us that prior to the revolution they were idle more than half the time, because they were not provided with raw material, and they complained bitterly of the treatment they had received in the days of the Tsar.

Whilst at Moscow my colleagues and I were asked to attend a delegate meeting of the Workmen's and Soldiers' Council.   The Mayor loaned us his motor car because it was raining heavily.   On our arrival there I found there must have been between three and four hundred delegates present.   One very fine-looking young man in a velvet jacket, during his speech kept shouting in his own language: "Make peace, make peace at any price!"

It was at this meeting I found out that the German and Russian soldiers were fraternising together on the frontier, and that twenty battalions from the German Army had been transferred to some other front.   There was not much fighting in consequence.   About two days afterwards, in the Russian newspapers, mention was made that these same twenty battalions had given our soldiers at Passchendale a rough time.

At the close of the meeting, my colleagues and myself were informed by the chauffeur that the car which had been lent to us by the Mayor had been stolen, with the result that we had to walk home, and arrived there about 12 o'clock at night.   I came to the conclusion that some one in collusion with the chauffeur had

" pinched " the car. The Mayor, however, issued a reward of 600 roubles to any one who could give any information about the stolen car.

I had another experience at Minsk, at a meeting organised by the Workmen's and Soldiers' Council, which consisted partly of farmer peasants from the surrounding communes. I must say I have never seen such an interesting spectacle.

In all the towns we passed through we met various generals and dined with them, and I remember at Minsk, when we were dining with one of the generals, a little Russian fellow had been chosen to follow us. Whilst we were having a chat with the officers we found out through our interpreter that this Russian delegate was " gingering up " all the junior officers, and pumping poison into their minds to persuade the soldiers in the battalion to refuse to do any more fighting.

We got back to Moscow on May Day, just in time to witness a great demonstration that was held in what is now known as the Red Square, outside the Kremlin walls. While we were in Russia the famous Leeds Conference was being held in England, representative of all working-class organisations, at which Ramsay MacDonald took a prominent part.

This Conference had sent a telegram to the Central Council of Workers, Soldiers and Sailors, in which they said that the delegation were Government agents. This caused us a lot of trouble, for on the Continent the term " Government agent " means Government " spy." This news had been well disseminated in Russia and was causing us a lot of trouble, until the matter was cleared up and explained in a telegram from our late Comrade H. M. Hyndman.

Arriving in Petrograd on the return journey, we again met the Soldiers' and Workmen's Council, who were in the midst of a debate on the question of whether they would take part in the new Government that was being formed by Kerensky. On this same night there arrived from Geneva, a man who was to be the greatest of his age and the real leader of the Russians; this was no other than Lenin. He made a speech which lasted over two hours, but when the vote was taken it was found that he had not been elected a member of the Government. Lenin had, however, started his work in preparation for the real revolution and a stable and suitable form of Government for Russia.

Kerensky's unstable administration has passed away, and though Lenin is dead, the administration that he gave the Russian people lives and grows stronger daily. If Kerensky had been a firmer man and of stronger character than he was, if he had been guided by the desires of the masses and not influenced by the politicians and reactionaries, he might have saved Russia much of the trouble and suffering that she has had to pass through.

I met him several times in Petrograd with the British Ambassador, Sir George Buchanan, and was struck with his charming manner and what I took to be his humanitarian ideals. Before leaving Petrograd we learnt that the propaganda of Lenin and his colleagues was spreading rapidly through the workshops and factories and among the fighting forces.

On the return journey our ship was guarded by two British gunboats, for the submarine war was then at its height.

On my return to England from Russia I was asked by Mr. Lloyd George, then Prime Minister, to report to him upon the Russian situation. I went at once to 10, Downing Street. When Lloyd George came in he told me he had just had an interview with the King, who, he said, was anxious to see me. I asked, " When ? " and he replied, " At once." I said, " Tell him I'll come right away."

I was wearing my ordinary office clothes at the time, and had no opportunity of going home and changing, for in addition to the message that Lloyd George gave me, a communication had come from Lord Stamfordham asking me to proceed to Buckingham Palace as speedily as possible. I jumped into a taxi and directed the driver, who seemed a little amazed when I said, " Buckingham Palace, quick."

On my arrival at the palace, I told Lord Stamfordham the object of my visit. He said he knew all about it. I then told him this was my first visit to the Palace, and the first call of its kind I had made upon His Majesty.

I also told Lord Stamfordham that I had been led to understand that one had to do a lot of bowing and scraping when in the King's presence. " When you enter the room," he replied, " wait until His Majesty arrives. All you will have to do is to stand up and say, ' Good morning, your Majesty, I am very pleased to see you.' "

I carried out these instructions when I met the King, and he said to me, " Please sit down, Mr. Thorne. I want to have a chat with you about your experiences in Russia. I expect they were very interesting." For over half an hour I sat chatting with the King, telling him of all I had seen and heard, and particularly of the way the soldiers had been starved and kept short of ammunition.

The King seemed greatly disturbed about the famous Leeds Conference, and asked me if I knew anything about it. I said, " Yes, I know all about it. I've read all the proceedings." I also told him about the telegram that had been sent from the Conference that made the Russians think that we were spies, and he was amused at my story of some of the incidents that had happened over this message.

" Do you think any ill will come from this Conference at Leeds and the decisions that were made there ? " the King asked me. " No," I said ; " I've seen these things happen before many times in days gone by, and in my humble judgment there will never be a physical violent revolution in this country. But there will have to be many political and industrial changes within the course of the next few years."

This seemed to relieve his mind, and he spoke to me in a most homely and pleasant way. I was very pleased.

I had expected to meet a haughty, stand-offish man with a highly-polished University twang ; but I found him a very different person. When the interview came to an end we wished one another " Good morning and good luck."

Shortly after this visit, with O'Grady and Sanders I prepared a secret report for the War Cabinet of what we had learnt from our visit to Russia.

Many people were anxious to know about my experiences, and I was asked to speak at a great number of meetings on the subject. I gave one of these lectures at Newport, in South Wales, and then went on to Pontypridd, where I stayed at an hotel called " The Farmers' Arms." While there, at about 8.30 in the evening, I heard a terrible row in the tap-room, so I went in to investigate, and found between fifteen and twenty colliers having a battle royal.

The two men who had started the quarrel decided to meet next morning on a nearby mountain side and fight the matter out. I decided to see the fight and, with the proprietor of the place, started early for the scene of battle. A most amazing thing took place before the fight started. There must have been a couple of hundred colliers present, and before the ring was made they crowded together and sang Welsh hymns for a quarter of an hour.

The fight was a short but desperate affair, the bigger man winning in about ten minutes. Afterwards the two combatants shook hands and, I was told, managed to get happily drunk together.

Just before the war, as a member of the Asylum Committee of the West Ham Borough Council, I paid a visit to the Brentwood Asylum for the purpose of the periodical inspections that the committee have to carry out. While looking round I came across two large bins of sugar. One was full of very common sugar, while the other was of a much better quality. I called the attention of the superintendent to this, and asked the reason.

He told me that the inferior grade was for the patients, and the better quality for the attendants and officials. I immediately said that this was wrong—what was good enough for the attendants was not too good for the patients, and this practice was immediately stopped.

In the laundry of the asylum I came across one of the inmates, a big stout woman, who, when she saw me, jumped up on to a box and started talking as though delivering an outdoor speech. The gist of her talk was that she was the Queen of England.

As soon as the war broke out I wanted to take my share in the work that had to be done. I joined the West Ham Volunteer Force, and was given the rank of Lieut.-Colonel.

I shall never forget my first public appearance in this capacity. My uniform, the details of which had caused some very anxious moments at the tailor's—and incidentally on my following pay day—was finally ready for the event. Straps were cleaned, buttons polished, and my home generally turned upside down in getting ready for parade. Even the bacon for breakfast got burned during an argument as to whether I should wear spurs or not. I had no idea that the dress regulations of the Army were so exacting ; but the united efforts of relatives and friends who had some knowledge in these matters enabled me to emerge from my home in full martial array, much to the amazement of my neighbours.

Sir Francis Lloyd, Commander-in-Chief of the Home Forces, was to inspect my battalion, and for once I felt very sheepish. When I arrived on parade, I asked the captain what I should have to do, and he replied, " You will be on parade behind the colonel. Whatever he does, you follow suit."

Unfortunately, I was placed in front of the colonel, and had to take sly looks round to see what he was doing—no easy matter when standing at " attention." The climax of my discomfiture, however, came at the taking of the salute. I noticed that men near me were saluting, and, inwardly feeling pleased that I had noticed their movement, I saluted also. But, remembering the captain's advice, I still thought it advisable to watch the colonel.

Turning round, I saw that he was standing fast at attention. I dropped my hand hastily, and immediately noticed the colonel's hand go up. I became a kind of human semaphore in my efforts to do the right thing. Just as the saluting was coming to an end I realised that I had been giving the salute with the wrong hand !

I had my photograph taken in full uniform, and when they were circulated I was very pleased with them, until it was pointed out to me that the buckle on my belt was on the wrong side of the leather, a breach of Army Regulations. The skill of the photographer, who altered the negative before much harm was done, was a small but happy blessing. The troubles I had in such matters caused me to welcome the Armistice, when I hoped my military career would terminate, but on tendering my resignation I learnt that the rule was " Once a colonel, always a colonel." I have never heard any more of my resignation.

While I was an officer some of my subordinates at my office got the idea that it was part of King's Regulations and my duty continually to dispense hospitality to them. They argued that it was *infra dig.* for them to pay their share of anything when the colonel was present.

Once, and only once, four of them came to see me on business at the House of Commons. It was early evening, and they gave me a broad hint that I should stand them a dinner to celebrate my commission. Feeling in generous mood I took the hint. Towards the end of the meal I was obliged to leave the dining-room and go to the debating chamber, so I arranged with the catering staff for the bill to be given me the next day. The next day carelessly jingling some loose silver in my pocket I asked for the bill, thinking that my friends had just had an ordinary meal.

I asked what time they had left, and the waitress told me it was rather late. This set me thinking, and on opening the bill I was thunderstruck at the figure in the pounds' column. They had, indeed, done themselves well ; it had been a real night out for them at my expense !

During the war I met Lord Kitchener several times, both at the War Office and in the House of Commons. He came to the House several times to meet the trade union leaders and explain to them the difficult and awkward position in which he found himself owing to a lack of munitions and shortage of man power. Kitchener had several meetings with the members in the House of Commons when certain misunderstandings and criticisms arose. He wanted to meet the members face to face and explain the exact position.

He was a charming man, and despite his great responsibility and the amount of work he had to do I enjoyed several brief conversations with him.

The horrors of war, its futility and waste, were driven home to me both in my military and everyday life. Though we won the war we are still paying very dearly for our victory. Poverty, unemployment and misery among large masses of people are still as rampant as ever, and, if anything, worse than before our victory. Thousands of people are still living in slums and suffering from want of houses. It is my earnest hope that the war has taught us all its uselessness, and that we shall learn the lesson of talking peace and of using peaceful methods to settle our international differences in future.

A great advocate of peace is the Countess of Warwick, and I am thankful for my many meetings and associations with her. Often I attended meetings at a flat she had in Carlisle Mansions, where she used to gather together the advanced thinkers of the Labour Movement. Each year she gave me wonderful help and assistance with my " Children's Sunday " work on the Sunday prior to Trade Union Congress week. On one of these occasions, at Bath, the town's lighting failed, and the Countess and I held our meeting in a tent by candlelight.

The Countess often addressed meetings for me. I remember one at the dock gates, near the Custom House, where we had to use an old waggon as a platform and ginger beer boxes for steps. The dockers were surprised to see a woman of title speaking in the East End on behalf of a Labour candidate. Once, when the Countess was addressing a meeting from the steps of my committee room in the Barking Road, such a huge crowd gathered that the trams had to be stopped. There were many children present, and the police came to stop the meeting because it was holding up the traffic.

The Countess afterwards said to me : " Mr. Thorne, these two meetings have been a most interesting and extraordinary experience for me. I was a little bit nervous, especially when speaking to the dockers, and as for those poor children, it looks to me as though they could do with a jolly good feed and some clothing to put on their poor little bodies."

I told her that there were thousands more like them in Tidal Basin, Custom House, Old Canning Town, Silvertown, and other parts of the East End, and that they were the constant thought of myself, George Lansbury, and all the other Labour workers in that part of London.

The hospitality of the Countess was unlimited. She invited my wife and I to spend a fortnight in an old English cottage alongside Easton Lodge. It was a very pleasant two weeks. Every morning the Countess would visit us, bringing fruit and other delicacies. One day she took us for a drive to Clacton-on-Sea, and on the road we ran over a chicken. My wife was very sorry about this ; but the Countess remarked, " It is just a chicken, and it will do some one good."

I met Lord Warwick at a flower show at Easton Lodge at which the Countess had asked me to speak. Lord Warwick asked me whether I thought the Countess was making any progress in her fight for the feeding of school children. I told him that I thought she was making very good progress and that it would not be long before an Act of Parliament was passed giving local authorities power to feed the children.

He replied : " I am heart and soul in the movement myself. I think it is a crying shame that any of the poor children should be starving in a wealthy country like ours."

On an organising tour with Jack Jones, M.P., we had a meeting at Coventry, where the Countess was also a speaker. She invited Jones and myself to stay at Warwick Castle for the night. She did not go back with us as she was going on to Birmingham. At the castle we had a very good meal and plenty to drink, and after looking over the castle we adjourned to bed. We had separate bedrooms.

My bed was exceedingly comfortable, and the next morning the attendant said to me : " Mr. Thorne, do you know whose bed you've been sleeping in ? " I told him I did not, but that it was very comfortable. " Well," he said, " you have been sleeping in Lord Warwick's bed ! "

The Countess once told me that she spent a great deal of money in helping the Labour Movement, and I have already mentioned how her income was reduced when she espoused the Labour faith. I only wish we had a few thousand more women in the country with the same earnestness, ability and intelligence as the Countess of Warwick.

Many adventures have come my way during my political work, both inside and outside the House of Commons.

From the early 'eighties I have taken an active interest in Parliamentary General Elections. In those early days political fights were usually the signal for physical fights between the opposing parties in the constituencies, and in these I was compelled to take part on many occasions.

At one election I met the great land expert and author, Mr. Henry George. He was a man worth meeting. He presented me with copies of his books, giving me " Progress and Poverty " especially, in appreciation of my organisation of the Gas Workers and General Labourers.

The coming of Keir Hardie to the division, now represented by Jack Jones and myself, met with opposition from many people, particularly the Liberals and Radicals, who organised meetings for the purpose of attempting to introduce a Liberal candidate into the division. We promptly counter attacked, broke up the meetings, and threw many of our opponents into a ditch that ran near by the place where their meetings were held.

Keir Hardie received the support of all the Labour groups, Home Rulers, Nonconformists, temperance workers, working women and children's groups, and the unemployed in the 1892 election, who held united demonstrations in his support. The result of the election was that Hardie was returned with a majority of more than 1,200 over his Conservative opponent. He had been despised by many, including a number of trade union leaders, because of his advanced ideas, and his election caused quite a stir.

After his election I rode with Hardie to the Houses of Parliament in a waggonette, followed by a band and a procession of his supporters. He wore a cloth cap, and his entrance to the chamber in this unconventional headgear was regarded by many old and dignified members as an impertinence and a slight on the House.

Lloyd George put in an appearance in the division at the next election in an attempt to get a Liberal candidate adopted. He was unsuccessful in his efforts, but so was Keir Hardie, who, in turn, was defeated by his old Conservative opponent.

Between this and the next election misunderstandings arose as to who was to be the next working-class Parliamentary candidate. Keir Hardie declared that " Will

Thorne is the only man I will stand down for," and he wrote me the following letter, which, in addition to explaining the confusion that had arisen, will have historic and personal interest to many :—

"You may remember that after my defeat last time I announced that had I won the seat it was not my intention to have again contested it. That still remains the position so far as I am concerned. I do not require to explain to you my reason for this ; it is self evident. All over the country I have been met with the taunt by Liberals that, having betrayed the working men of South-West Ham, they would not again have me as their candidate, and my withdrawal from the constituency would lend colour to this assertion. For that reason and for that alone I should have liked to have once more had the opportunity of contesting the seat. I think I understand your position and am quite sure that it is prompted, as your action always has been, as much by personal friendship to myself as by a desire to help on the movement in which we are both engaged. No matter what the final outcome may be, it will not make any difference to our personal friendship.

"I feel very strongly that the opposition is a manufactured one, and that once I was fairly before the electorate again there would be the same rallying of the forces as there was before. Of course, if Hill is the candidate, it would stand very hard with the Socialist, as despite his past he would be able to command a very strong following and make the issue extremely doubtful. Apart from him, I believe the seat to be perfectly safe for me, or for you. I am being pressed very strongly to go to Leicester, where the chances of a win are exceedingly good, also to the Chester-le-Street Division of Durham, which I should dearly love to fight as the Radical there is Sir James Joicey, one of the very worst types of politicians. You said in your last letter that you would write me concerning the position, and I would be glad if you would take a few minutes to do so, so that I may know exactly where we stand.

" Yours faithfully,
(*Signed*.) " J. KEIR HARDIE."

The situation between Hardie and myself was cleared up and I was invited to be the candidate at the next election, after my Executive Council had given me permission. When the election took place, in 1900, I was defeated ; but we kept the political machinery working hard, and in 1906 I became a Member of Parliament for the first time, defeating my Conservative opponent by over 5,000 votes.

It was at this election that I assisted Jack Jones in his fight at Camborne. I have a constant reminder of this election in a damaged knee that still gives me pain.

I was on the platform with Jack Jones and Joe Terrett. Before the meeting had actually started a crowd broke open the doors, and when the meeting began a chorus of booing and shouting was set up by the rowdies. Missiles were thrown about and the platform was rushed.

Jones and Terrett jumped off the back of the platform, but I was hemmed in and had to jump into the middle of the crowd, who immediately started to punch and kick me unmercifully. The crowd was shouting, " Take him to the pond ! " I was being hustled along, as I thought to the pond, but I had been surrounded by a group of mining students, who, just as we were passing an hotel, slipped me in and shut the door.

Fortunately a nurse was attending the publican's wife and she bathed and bandaged my injuries. By this time a big crowd had gathered outside the hotel, but the publican got me away and I reached my lodgings safely.

On the advice of a police inspector we cancelled further meetings in Camborne ; and the rowdies, not to be deprived of their sport, proceeded to upset the meetings of the Tory candidate.

I still feel the effects of the terrible kicking I received. When the weather is bad I am stricken with a slight form of paralysis in the knee, which causes me to limp.

CHAPTER XII

My maiden speech in the House of Commons stands out vividly in my memory.

Lloyd George had been making a long, ambiguous speech, full of high-sounding phrases, which satisfied no one. Unemployment was rampant, and the Labour Party had decided to raise the matter on the adjournment. I was selected to open the debate, and when I rose to my feet I thought I should sink through the floor. For a few seconds, that seemed like years, I felt as though I was chloroformed. Every eye in the Chamber seemed to be fixed upon me. I imagined that every one's ears were three or four times their normal size, and that all were reaching out to catch the words I felt I could never get out of my mouth.

I stuttered and stammered for a moment, and then recovered and started talking in my best outdoor style. Such a style may not be suitable for the House of Commons ; but I had something to say—hard, human facts about thousands of starving unemployed. I hurled these tragic tales of hunger and misery at my opponents, and they listened, but I was glad when I had finished my speech and sat down to a cheerful burst of applause, some of which came from my opponents.

The late Will Crooks, Keir Hardie, and George Barnes took up the burden of my tale. They were replied to by my one-time colleague, John Burns—who was then a Cabinet Minister—as President of the Local Government Board. He went out of his way to make a ferocious attack upon the Labour members, and would give no assurances that the Government would bring in a Bill to deal with unemployment.

It was during this Parliament that I was the central figure in an incident that I believe to be without precedent. A heated debate was in progress on the Finance Bill. Tempers were ruffled, and speakers were being subjected to a continuous fire of interruption. Mr. John Hodge, who was sitting next to me, was interrupting Captain Pretyman. I turned to him and said : " You had better shut up, for there's going to be trouble " ; but he persisted in his interruptions.

Suddenly Lord Winterton rose in his seat and, turning to the Chairman, said, " I wish to draw your attention to the fact that the honourable member for West Ham [myself] is in an unfit state to take part in the debate."

The blood rushed to my head. I jumped up and shouted back : " I am as sober as you are, my young friend ! " Amidst cries of " Withdraw " that were directed at Lord Winterton, the Chairman said : " I think the noble lord's remark was quite unjustified and he must withdraw it."

I was still on my feet, and shouted : " He ought to have the words rammed down his throat." Lord Winterton said that in his sincere opinion he thought I was not in a fit state to take part in the debate, but as the Chairman had ruled that I was, he would withdraw what he had said.

At this stage Keir Hardie, on a point of order, asked whether Lord Winterton's statement was a withdrawal, to which the latter replied, " Unreservedly." I was still excited, and said, " If he is not prepared to withdraw I will call him a liar." The Chairman told me that I must not call a noble lord a liar, and I replied, " He is an absolute liar. I am as sober as any man in the House."

I had used an unparliamentary expression, and the Chairman asked me to withdraw the word " liar."

This I refused to do, upon which I was told that I must withdraw from the proceedings. I immediately rose and walked out of the Chamber ; but as I went I turned to Lord Winterton and shouted, " Now you walk out and see if you're as sober as I am."

After I had left, Keir Hardie pleaded with the Chairman to allow me to return. Earl Winterton, as a result of Keir Hardie's appeal, said he apologised unreservedly ; but it was technically impossible, according to the rules of the House, for my suspension to be withdrawn by the Chairman.

The following day it was realised by all parties that I had been grossly slandered by Winterton, and, in consequence of this feeling, Mr. Asquith moved an unusual motion, to the effect that all record of my suspension be expunged from the journal of the House. He said many nice things about me, and his motion was seconded by Mr. (now Lord) Balfour. The motion was agreed to without a division, and I was again a full-fledged Member of Parliament. In only two other cases have records been expunged from the minutes, once in the seventeenth century, and once in the last century in connection with Charles Bradlaugh.

I received a great amount of sympathy from my trade union friends. The General Council of my union was in session when a suitable resolution was moved and carried unanimously. Mr. J. R. Clynes, who spoke at the Council meeting, called the attention of the Chairman to " my unfit condition to take part in the business of the meeting." The words caused a roar of laughter, for this time they were true, because, following my usual custom, I had returned early from lunch, and was indulging in a peaceful nap which had continued longer than I had intended !

During all the years that I have been a Member of Parliament I have consistently tried to get legislation enacted that would improve the lot of the working class. I have been associated with Bills of all kinds, from nationalisation to cheap workmen's trains ; I have introduced deputations of all kinds and characters to Prime Ministers and Cabinet Ministers.

The usual share of experiences that come to a Member of Parliament have befallen me. During the agitation for women's suffrage, Miss Pankhurst came to the House of Commons to see me and to inquire, " What are you Labour people doing towards demanding an extension of the franchise ? " I told her that the Labour Party was not very strong and did not have time to do very much. She said : " At least you can kick up an infernal row and draw public attention to the question." I asked her whether she expected us to get tin whistles and other noise-making instruments, and she replied, " Certainly. Any old thing as long as you make a noise ! " When I told her that I did not propose to adopt her suggestion, she became very indignant and said, " You Labour men are like all the others . . . frauds." And that was the last time that I met Miss Pankhurst !

While this women's suffrage agitation was going on the women who were arrested were let out of prison under what was known as " The Cat and Mouse Act," and one night a woman in the Strangers' Gallery, as a gibe at this Act, caused quite a commotion in the House by throwing a large number of artificial mice into the chamber. On another occasion a man supporter of the suffragettes threw himself over the gallery on to the floor of the House, and had forcibly to be removed by the attendants.

I often met Horatio Bottomley in the House. As a member of the Kitchen Committee, I noticed several times that he was on the " defaulter's list," with several accounts outstanding for food and liquor consumed in his name.

The last time I spoke to him was in 1918, after he had been sworn in. He asked Lord Dalziel, myself, and a few others to have a drink with him. He always drank champagne, and on this occasion he opened several bottles. He always seemed a decent man socially ; but

I never knew anything about his commercial morality, which in the end landed him in gaol. Whenever he spoke in the House, he always reminded me of Charles Bradlaugh, whom I had often heard in my younger days.

When Lady Astor first became a Member of Parliament, she took a seat near me. Sir Joynson Hicks, by custom, had a prior right to the seat. He was on a visit to India at the time, and when he returned he demanded his seat back. Lady Astor, not wanting to quarrel with him, immediately gave it up, and was left without a regular position.

I at once made arrangements with my Labour colleagues to move along and make room for Lady Astor on the corner. This was agreed to, and Lady Astor thanked me heartily for what I had done.

We have had many talks together while we have been sitting side by side. One day I said to her : " I would not like to be in your house when you are out of temper ; I think you must be a fiery cat." She said to me appealingly, " Oh, don't say that, Mr. Thorne ! I can assure you I have not a violent temper, not nearly so violent as yours, according to what I've seen during the time I've been in the House."

After I had secured the corner seat for her, she sent me the following letter :—

" MY DEAR MR. THORNE,—

" I can't tell you how much I appreciate your courtesy and kindness in offering me your corner seat. I hope very much that I won't have to deprive you of it for long, but it does help me out of a very awkward situation just now—and I can never forget your kindness.

" Sincerely,
" NANCY ASTOR."

She has shown her appreciation in many other ways. Just after this incident she presented me with two gold-cased pencils and a beautiful diamond and pearl tie pin. When I was ill in Aberdeen, she sent me roses from her

own garden.   During my wife's illness she also sent her
fruit and flowers, as well as to my son when he was in
hospital at Falmouth.

My most intimate conversation with the Prince of
Wales was brought about by Lady Astor.   For some
time she had been making arrangements to entertain
the Prince, and one evening in the House of Commons
she asked me if I would like to dine with her on the
important occasion.   I agreed on one condition—that I
should be permitted to wear my everyday clothes.   Her
reply was that I could wear any clothes I liked.

I decided to go.   Members of the Government, including Lord Balfour and other distinguished persons,
attended.   Most of them wore their decorations.
Orders, honours, and medals flashed from almost every
breast, and there was I, amongst the glory and grandeur,
in my workaday clothes.

When I reached the house in St. James's Square,
several magnificent motor cars were lined up outside,
and crowds of people were waiting to see the guests
arrive.   I paused for a moment before I entered.
Finally I plucked up courage and, pushing through the
crowd, marched up to the door, conscious all the time
that I was a little out of place.

The door was opened by servants in gorgeous livery.
They looked at me in amazement, and I am sure they
wondered who I was.   My hat, stick, and coat were
taken, and I was escorted to the grand stairway, at the
top of which was Lady Astor, beautifully dressed and
crowned with a glittering diamond coronet.   She gave
me a hearty welcome and introduced me to several of
her friends.

The silvery notes of an Oriental gong summoned us
to dinner.   At the time I was speaking to Lady Astor's
sister.   I offered her my arm and escorted her to the
table, where Lady Astor had seated me near the Prince
of Wales.

Lord and Lady Astor are teetotalers ; but there was
an abundance of wines and spirits.   I was not aware

that my table companion, Lady Astor's sister, was also
a teetotaler, and during the course of the meal, when I
asked her if she would care to have some wine, her
ladyship raised a threatening finger to me lest I should
persuade her sister.

During the meal I was fascinated by the glitter of the
gems and the wondrous clothes of those about me. The
general atmosphere of luxury gave me a rosy glow. I
looked at the beautiful women around me and, turning
to Lady Astor's sister, remarked that the beauty of it
all reminded me of a song I had often heard sung in
the East End. She was curious to know what it was,
and finally persuaded me to hum the song I had in
mind.

> " Those lovely, lovely girls ;
> They have eyes like diamonds, teeth like pearls,
> I love 'em one and all ; stout, short, and tall.
> Oh, those beautiful, beautiful girls."

She was highly amused at the song, and I was almost
getting in the mood to sing other songs. I told her
there were many other similar ditties, and she was very
anxious to hear them ; but I only told her the words
of one I faintly remembered about a " hansom cab that
she might ride with me." Like all good things, the
dinner ended and she bade me good-night with the
hope that we should soon meet again.

After dinner we adjourned to another room, and
Lady Astor asked me if I would like to speak to the
Prince of Wales. I said I would be delighted, and we
were introduced. I reminded the Prince that we had
met before at a function at the offices of the London
County Council, and he told me he remembered the
occasion quite well.

Eventually our conversation turned to serious subjects. The Prince said to me : " Mr. Thorne, do you
think any serious trouble will arise in this country ? "

I replied : " No widespread trouble will take place
in this country, but there are bound to be labour
troubles from time to time for many years to come.

But please understand that practically all the Parliamentary Labour Party, including myself, are in favour of obtaining the social, economic, and industrial reforms we desire by constitutional methods."

The Prince thought for a moment, and then replied : " Well, no one can object to that."

We chatted for a little while longer, and then I bade him good-night, as I was anxious to get home to my wife, who was not very well at the time. Coming away I met many more guests, including Philip Snowden, who had not been invited to the dinner, and who was only just arriving for the reception.

I appreciated the kindness that Lady Astor intended in inviting me to this function, but I was not, nor have I ever been, anxious to make a regular practice to mingle in such society as I did on this occasion. I would rather lose my life than my consciousness that I am a member of the working class, and that I have been entrusted with the sacred duty and honour of fighting the class war until there is an equal distribution of the work and the wealth of the nation. I think that I can, as Kipling says, " Walk with kings, nor lose the common touch."

CHAPTER XIII

THE FUTURE

My story draws to a close. I realise that it is not complete in many ways. I make no claim to literary ability. I am a common man of the people, and my life has been one long round of years full of work, suffering, and struggle.

When I was asked to write my story, I hesitated, because such a task would be no easy one even for an educated man or a well-trained journalist. I was also faced with the fact that for the most part I would have to rely on my memory, and it would be a great feat for any one to remember the dates and details of all the activities, great and small, that I have engaged in. I do not boast unduly when I claim that there is hardly another man in the Labour Movement who has had such a varying and interesting life in all phases of the working-class movement as I have had.

What with the frailty of my memory, the lack of documents with which to refresh it, and the space limit to my story, I have omitted much. There are three main phases of the working-class movement. They are the industrial, political, and international, and for the last thirty or forty years no one will deny that I have played a prominent part in each phase, the part of the pivot around which these activities have revolved and enlarged.

For the last thirty-six years I have been general secretary of one of the greatest trade unions in the United Kingdom. It is generally assumed that such a position is handsomely paid and means a happy and comfortable existence. This might be true in some cases, but not in mine. Travelling about the country, I have received welcomes and rough-and-ready hospitality. I have slept in beds of all kinds—in garrets, cellars, and all manner of strange places. This was in the days when my wage was first £2 5s. a week, then £3, until the year 1920, when the annual conference of the union decided to change the basis of payment from that of a weekly wage to a salary of £700 a year.

I received this news under unusual circumstances. Whilst travelling to the Conference I felt rather unwell in the train, and, making light of the matter, merely sent a telegram to the hotel ordering some creature comforts. Being in great pain, I soon got to bed on arrival, but my friends insisted on calling in a doctor, who took a grave view and sought further medical advice.

It was found that I had acute appendicitis, and the only treatment was an immediate operation. This was performed, and I came through, but it was the nearest I have got to the shades yet. Needless to say, the Conference was obliged to go on without me ; but the extraordinary concern of the delegates for my welfare was very comforting.

They would cheer at the top of their voices each day in an endeavour to try and make me hear the sound at the nursing home where I was lying. But I certainly think it was the intimation of the advance in pay to £700 per year which greatly assisted in stimulating my holding on to life.

My luck did not last long, however, for, together with all my colleagues, I had to face the facts of lessened union membership following the end of the war, and the consequent depressed financial conditions. We all sacrificed £2 a week in July, 1922, and later a further drop of £1 10s. We have thus, as trade union officials, had a greater percentage of wages reduction than any other workers.

The fact that I have been elected to my present position by the democratic vote of the members of the union biennially since 1889 does not indicate any desire on their part to dispense with my services, nor have I ever wished to seek another berth. The tokens of good-will I have received, the kindly-worded messages that have been sent to me annually on my birthday, are more than symbols of the cordial feeling that exists between myself and the rank and file of the union.

One such token of appreciation came as a great surprise to me when in the twenty-fifth year of my office as general secretary, Mr. J. R. Clynes, M.P., casually remarked to me one day that the members of the union were to give me a complimentary dinner and a presentation in recognition of my long service. The war was then in progress, and it was thought that but a few members would be able to be present, and only a modest programme had been arranged at a club room near Charing Cross.

It turned out that the accommodation was absolutely inadequate, and many members were disappointed who were unable to attend. Of the gifts that I received on this occasion the one I value most was a magnificent illuminated address, in the following terms :—

TO

MR. WILL THORNE, M.P.

THE MEMBERS AND OFFICIALS OF THE NATIONAL
UNION OF GASWORKERS AND GENERAL
LABOURERS

ask you to accept the gifts herewith offered, to-gether with this expression of their grateful thanks for the devoted service you have rendered to the UNION as its Chief Secretary for Twenty-five Years.

During that time your responsible and varied labours have been discharged with marked ability and success, and any difficulty readily faced by you at the call of duty. The position attained by

the UNION and the substantial benefits procured
for its members have been due largely to your
untiring work in a post which all your colleagues
and friends fervently hope you will long continue
to fill.

J. R. CLYNES, *President.*
ARTHUR HAYDAY, *Vice-President.*
February 13th, 1915.

I am sure that there is not another trade union
official in the country who has had to deal with so many
strikes, lock-outs and other disputes as I have had to
in the last thirty-six years. There are many people who
think trade union officials like strikes. Personally I
hate them. They mean great anxiety and worry,
generally a heavy drain on financial resources, often
the cause of many complications, and quite often, in
the case of failure, men and women are left unemployed
" upon the stones."

My endeavour is always to get disputes settled without resorting to direct action ; but I recognise that the
workers must never give up the strike weapon, which is
their greatest power in the ceaseless class war. A study
of the industrial history of England will show that
practically all the improvements and reforms that have
been gained by the workers has been by the use of direct
action in some form or another, and I am certain that
if the trade union movement abandons this weapon,
wages and economic and industrial conditions would
immediately be worsened.

I confess that I have made many mistakes, but I
never had the opportunity of going to school, nor much
time for self-education. I do not remember how or
when I learnt to read and write. All my knowledge,
both general and of the great Trade Union and Labour
Movement, has been gained by practice, bitter experience, and by contact in my earlier years at meetings
and lectures with such men as Bernard Shaw, H. M.
Hyndman, Charles Bradlaugh, and other intellectuals

at the time. Such books as " Fabian Essays," that were presented to me by Graham Wallace and Sidney Webb, who inscribed the title page, " Progress and Poverty," also presented to me by the author, Henry George, have helped me to understand the fundamentals of economics and of working-class problems.

I can never forget, and I never want to forget, the brave, nameless people, both men and women, who, directly and indirectly, were responsible in the early days for putting me in the position that I now occupy, and helped me to gain the various honours that have been conferred on me in the fields of municipal activity, political work and in the trade union movement generally. I hope that I have never been guilty of a common ailment that occurs to many people when they become promoted to responsible positions, an ailment that is better known as " swelled head."

I have seen many such people who, immediately they receive the confidence of the workers, try to talk differently from their natural and usual method ; who try to ape the snobs of the possessing class. I am satisfied to be natural, even though I be rough and blunt, and sometimes brutally frank.

I have always called " a spade a spade," and have always found that a few plain, homely words are just as effective and eloquent as flowery, long-phrased speech. I confess to illtreating the King's English and an ignorance of grammar ; but, in spite of all this, my colleagues in the Trade Union Movement have frequently sought my services as their chief advocate of the workers' claims and rights before the most powerful of employers' associations.

My mis-pronunciation of the English language has been the subject of toleration and even humour among my friends. But it is sad and strange that a member of my own party took upon himself the task of ridiculing me in public for my faults in this direction.

This occurred after I had been asked to speak in the House of Commons on a certain Labour Party Bill. I know that many other members could have put up a better case than I did ; but I did my best, and was surprised later when my attention was called to what was described as my " unlettered ignorance and unfitness for Parliament," in a weekly Labour journal.

It was Philip Snowden who saw fit thus to sneer in public at a colleague's lack of educational polish, who, unlike myself, was born, and has always been, in comfortable circumstances. I felt his sneer as unworthy of a member of the party that is fighting and striving for the masses of the people. I was hurt bitterly at this uncalled for jibe, but, remembering his infirmity, I forgive the author.

This episode I can say is the only one in my career which really threatened to affect my spirit. It was in 1916, and the biennial conference of my union was being held in London at the time. A function had been arranged at a large restaurant, and I was called upon to propose the toast of " Success of the union." The room was packed with hundreds of people all anxious to hear me, but when I got up I was so depressed that I found myself absolutely unable to commence ; tears came to my eyes, and all that I could say was that if I was thought to be too ignorant for the Labour Movement I would not continue to be associated with it.

The whole audience rose *en masse* and cheered and sang until I recovered myself. After the lapse of years I bear no ill-will whatever to the individual concerned. I comfort myself with the reflection that, while his book learning might count in its proper perspective, that an education such as I have had can only be shaped in the school that really matters. This, at least, is right among the hard facts of life.

I think more of the kindness of those two humble souls in Swansea in their poor cottage, and the hospitality they gave me that I mentioned earlier in my story, than I do of the glittering and luxurious hospitality I have received, and also described, from the aristocracy. It is towards this great discrepancy between those that have and those that have not that I have always tried to direct my efforts with a view to bringing about a more equal distribution of the necessities and good things of life.

I do not believe, however, like some people that this can only be secured by violent changes, involving lots of life and bloodshed. On the other hand, I do not believe that we should be blindly loyal at all times. Criticism, honest, healthy criticism of one's associates and colleagues, is often necessary. It is essential to the progress and development of any and every organisation. On more than one occasion I have been called the "bad boy of the Labour Party," and several times I was reported by the secretary of the Labour Party to my Executive Council for not acting and working in accordance with the Parliamentary Labour Party.

I was not satisfied with the way the party was working, and was one of a small group of Labour members that got together in the House of Commons because of this. If necessary I shall do the same thing again, if I feel at any time that my party ceases to recognise the class struggle and its one real aim, the emancipation of the working class.

The running sands of time have brought me gladness and sadness. My son Karl, named in memory of Karl Marx, was taken from me, and as Fate would have it he was my favourite child. I have also lost my second wife—my helpmate and companion for many years. She was a real companion, and had I the skill of a poet in using words I could find none that would express what I feel about the loss of this beautiful soul. She was passionately fond of flowers and spent many hours in the garden. She would seldom pick them for our own house ; but often for other people. She would say that they gave the most pleasure to a greater number of people growing in the garden than if they were cut and in the house.

During the thirty years of our married life I had many ups and downs, all of which she shared with me. She was a grandmother and a thrifty and economical Chancellor of the Household Exchequer. Her foresight was revealed to me in a way I had never realised when, after her death, I found that she had left me £450, which she had saved and of which I knew nothing.

We must all follow along that dark and unknown road. Perhaps it may not be so dark as we have been led to believe, and I am sure it cannot be worse than what I and millions of workers throughout the world daily endure. I have been asked many times when I am going to retire, but while there is breath and life within me I shall continue the fight I started many years ago.

I can never forget the horror of my childhood days and the misery and suffering I have seen, and if I can leave the world a better place than I found it I shall die content.

The future is with the young workers. Let them continue to agitate, to educate and to organise. " Workers of the world unite ; you have nothing to lose but your chains ! " There is a world of freedom, beauty and equality to gain, where every one will have an opportunity to express the best that is in them for the benefit of all, making the world a place more to our heart's desire and the better to dwell in.

THE END.

PRINTED IN GREAT BRITAIN BY THE WHITEFRIARS PRESS, LTD.,
LONDON AND TONBRIDGE.

INDEX